COWBOYS
CAN CRY

Nick Dale

ISBN 979-8-88832-961-0 (paperback)
ISBN 979-8-88832-962-7 (digital)

Christian Faith Publishing
832 Park Avenue
Meadville, PA 16335
www.christianfaithpublishing.com

Printed in the United States of America

Introduction

At fifty-one, I found the space to look at the story of my life, the story that I had constructed. I say I found the space, but really the universe delivered me a rude awakening, a real slap that pushed me to create that space. What happened as a result can only be described as a horrifically glorious unraveling of my imprint and how I have interpreted that and then built on top of it. What I have begun to find out as a result of this forced introspection has been nothing short of sobering but liberating at the same time. Make no mistake—deconstructing a story that I have really put my back into for all of this time has at times been nakedly harrowing, and in those moments, the bravest thing I could do was just hang on and believe in the credence of the transformation that was on the other side of this naked examination. I chose to throw myself into this discovery wholeheartedly, arming myself with all the knowledge I can, marinating in the idea of how faulted my story has been, but heeding this innate knowing in the bottom of my belly: that in order to reconstruct, I needed to go all the way back to the foundation and rebuild from there.

This inward journey has had all the elements of *The Lord of the Rings*: days of bright sunshine and hope, mixed with the intensity of the badlands, and black clouds hanging over my sanity. Dark nights spent awake in the early hours terrified the hairs on my neck, standing rigid in attention. Rumination of thoughts, of how wrong I had got this all, then the even darker thoughts that are brought on by the deep rooted unconscious self-loathing. It's those nights that have called me to write this book. The grand hope is that it could provide anyone that honors me in reading it with a hit of hope, a tonic of courage to begin the journey of healing. A knowing that even in the most hopeless of landscapes, we have the tools to rise out of those depths and transform. We have an army of universal soldiers ready to fight with and for us. All they ask is that we embark on that journey inward, ask the questions, accept the answers, and just be present in each moment, whether it be holding on or living in the power of epiphanies, basking in the living of *now*.

Full disclaimer: I do not prescribe to being the most talented writer, but nevertheless feel called to write my story. This is my purpose to serve. We men have different narratives that society has placed on us, and we then have willingly just piled on more expectations. My generation became totally adept at pushing things deep and locking them away. Grit and perseverance, our constructed badges of honor, which mostly meant to suffer in silence and create methods of appearing strong, everything is good. My hope is that my story can break some of this toxic masculinity down so that I don't imprint my son with the same coldness with which to face life.

I thank you in advance for reading. Soldier on; do it deeply and honestly. What lies on the other side is a loosening of the tummy and a rediscovery of your inner self that leads to a life of freedom and abundance.

Chapter 1

The Day

Put simply, I was not listening or was not sure how to, either in a literal sense or an internal sense. I had crafted and cultivated my story and I jumped into it with an unerring dedication, never questioning whether this story was correct or if there was any other way. I wrapped this construct in a cemented coat of nobility and plowed forward. Buying in completely to the unwritten badges of honor of the time—first to arrive, last to leave, eighteen-hour days—all in pursuit of the trappings of what society saw as the signs of making it. The more elusive these seemed to be, the harder I pushed, all the while building the huge granite block on the inside, shutting down any aspects of being that did not serve this end. What this really meant was that I was engaging every day in a kind of justified self-preservation, judging myself of the perceived results, or really, the lack thereof. The societal narrative of hard work being the cure for all; believe me, the only real self-definition I allowed myself was work ethic, unrivaled.

This I have since come to realize just bedded in scarcity, self-loathing, and ultimately, survival mode. These are all unsustainable states and really damaging, even though I gave it a good attempt. I would have to go to bed at night with this identity that whether I heeded or not was not in sync, the public results out there in the world were average at best, but I kept banging my head on the same wall. Part of my story was to be relentless and your break will come. But something had to give, and that moment came on a random day out of the blue in a confusingly brutal way. The universe definitely got my attention—I have been listening ever since!

Now to write what it was that got me listening and the extreme attention of my insides. I will hopefully do the total upheaval of this day justice in service to trying to alleviate the stigma that is still attached to mental health. It needs to be said that the descriptions that we give to some of the more prevalent mental health issues today, in my view, seriously undermine the sheer terror of experiencing one of these episodes. Panic attacks and anxiety just somehow do not give any true detail of what it feels like. Anyone having gone through anything on the mental health scale, who has felt that level of hopelessness, the infinite nature of something afflicting your mind, the gnawing thought that you are somehow broken, knows the true loneliness of that place. My own contrived definition of strength meant that I had looked at the whole mental health debate from afar and had pompously given it the label of weakness. My manhood refused to think that I would ever fall foul of such indulgence until that day.

This day started out normally. Pamela, my wife, was away on a business trip, so I had stayed home on Dad duty. The usual morning: frenetic, I dropped my son off at school and went home looking forward to the stillness of the house for the next couple of hours. I popped on the easiness of daytime TV as I "worked from home." At this point nothing was amiss. Then out of nowhere a recurring ruminating thought began to loop in my mind. *You are hurting your family.*

Even though this was disturbing and unusual, I tried pushing it away as ridiculous, and of course, the more I tried to deny it, it just kept coming on stronger. I mean this was literally hair-raising. The more I explored and tried to outthink this evil little voice, the louder it got—an internal scream which had me squirming. Rumination is what the pros call it—kinda like playing your newly found favorite song on repeat, over and over. Taking control and slowly but very surely hijacking your identity with a healthy helping of irrationality, creeping ever closer to the bounds of your sanity.

But I had a plan. I figured I could outsmart this newfound foe and divert my attention. Let's get a haircut, get out into the world, interact in normality, and all will be good again. Big mistake. I sat in the chair of my usual barber, hoping this familiarity and her proneness to incessant chatter would fix all. Except my ruminating friend just simply upped the ante. *You are a danger to everyone*, over and over again, drowning out anything else.

I can only describe the white-knuckle experience that haircut was. For the entire thirty minutes, all I wanted to do was run, and I mean *run* anywhere as fast as I could as far as I could. Thinking about the feeling this thought created because in those moments I believed them, I scanned the other patrons sitting blissfully in their chairs and truly thought I was a danger to them. This was the purest of flight mode I had ever felt, but I hung on, all the while trying to appear completely normal on the outside, just waiting for the relief of being out in the car park into the safety of my truck. Only to find that nowhere was safe from this sneering voice.

One more chore to do: pick my son up from school. *You are hurting your family*. At this point, I am not going to lie. I was questioning my sanity. Something is broken, and truthfully, I am not a talented enough writer to really articulate how this felt, the suddenness of it, and what if it was true. *You are hurting your family*. With this mystifying crescendo in my head, I had to navigate the vagaries of a school parking lot, all the while truly feeling and believing that I was a danger. I felt totally cornered. Everywhere I turned felt like a dead end. My little guy bounded into my arms, and the tonic of the hug got me home, my sanctuary, except the enemy was within. No escape.

Then my in-laws arrived home with visiting out-of-state family in tow, just more people that I was a danger to. I clung onto my rational side, this heavyweight fight between the rational and irrational waging war on my sanity. The rational voice was on the ropes, taking body shots and uppercuts. *Run*. This level of internal alert was tantamount to a wooly mammoth charging me in my own home. I sought solitude in my room, googled what was happening, and *boom*, there it was: a digital hazmat suit. My self-diagnosis just signaled how in trouble I was. This time I heeded the call and I ran. This is when the suicide ideations kicked in. If I was truly hurting my family, then what was the point of living? There is no word in our language that describes the lonely terror of a moment like this.

I am in my truck, tears streaming down my face, just driving nowhere in particular—just far away! I make the call to my wife. She answers, sunny bright, happy to hear from me, then I feel her snap like a Marine to attention—my husband crying; this has never happened! Her laser focus, the beginning of an antidote.

"Babe, I don't know what's happening to me." I manage to spit out through the panicked sobbing. "I'm going to drive my truck off a cliff. I think I am broken!" The shame I felt in those utterances, the weakness.

That calm compassionate voice steered me toward the emergency room. "I am here, babe. You are not broken. You just need help." Honestly, I believe that my wife saved my life that day. I have written this paragraph in a staccato-like rhythm on purpose because these are completely chaotic frenetic moments, but also to indicate the soothing calm Pamela instinctively adopted. If any of you ever have the misfortune of fielding a call like this, try to remain cool, calm, and collected. It is truly the beginning of healing at that moment.

I arrived at the emergency room while my wife booked her flight home. "I am coming, babe."

The attendant nurse took me and tried to distract my rumination while I went through the tightrope of questions. "Did you plan anything?"

"*No!*" I screamed. I am a normal guy. This has come from nowhere—the great heist! Then I was pumped into a zombie state with both an oral and drip of lorazepam! In my haze, I was front and central to all of the goings on in a busy emergency room. This is where I experienced both stigma and hope at the hands of a pandemic-ravaged staff. I was placed right in front of the nurse station—I can only assume for direct observation, given the perceived danger I presented.

I watched as a man refused care and the police were promptly called, all the while the drugs had taken effect and I was floating in a haze, but at the same time lucid, so I could hear snippets of conversations around me. The staff was unfiltered, which was for the most part, deeply cynical and in some sense, uncaring. I heard a nurse refer to me as acting "loopy" in a tone that made me feel she was disbelieving of my reason for being there and that I somehow wanted to be there. I really felt the stigma of mental health in that moment, as if there was some type of stereotypical person that went through mental health crises, and because I did not fit the bill, I must somehow be some kind of faker. This sat with me for months after, as well as the Doc on duty exclaiming to me that I was just not the kind of person that had these thoughts or went through this—all of which made me feel like I was broken, unfixable!

But then at the change of shift, my own personal Florence Nightingale appeared in the form of a northern England accent, which comforted me as it is my lineage. She inquired as to what was going on with me and then took the time to come and sit with me and just talk things through. She told me her story. She spoke about her recovery. She gave me a road map of what to do once the emergency room discharged me, but what she really did was give me a speck of hope, just a speck. I was not an anomaly and there was a way out. She will never know what that small moment of compassion did for me. I assume she had chosen this vocation in order to have that very impact, but she had none of the jaded cynicism that the others displayed. Hope and stigma were the cocktails I was served, and then discharged without any diagnosis, any real understanding of what had just happened to me, a bottle of lorazepam clutched in my hand and a desolate nuclear reality to walk out into.

A discovery that I made in this process is that the emergency room by function looks to fix the most pronounced symptoms. In my case, that was reducing me to a zombie. But what they don't do—well, at least not in my experience—is provide a diagnosis, even a glimpse of understanding of what is going on. Now a broken arm is self-explanatory, but a mental episode not only can be so foreign to the person going through it. Honestly, it seemed pretty foreign to the emergency room. Sure, they had procedures in place for this kind of thing, but these were wrapped in a clinical almost dismissive manner.

There are learnings here. If someone had just said to me, "Hey, don't worry. You are safe here. We see this often," that would have given me another speck of hope and brought another little bit of calm. Instead, I was made to feel like a medical anomaly, which only intensified the panic. Of course, that was what I went through and may not be the norm. Either way, we should do our best to inject as much hope and compassion into these mental health procedures.

Chapter 2

WTF

That moment when your entire life is turned upside down, your identity gone, replaced by an unwelcome fragility out of nowhere. My generation of men were just not equipped to handle this kind of absolute desolation, the vulnerability required to even look at this without the scream just screeching, "You are weak!" In my world, cowboys did not cry, but more to the point, cowboys did not feel—not on purpose anyway. Right then as I walked out of that emergency room, I was completely answerless—a void, empty, lost, changed forever in the blink of an eye.

I waited outside for my father-in-law to pick me up, building up every ounce of something so that I could put on an outward brave face. I was awash with shame, fear, and extreme embarrassment. My world had changed completely. WTF? My entire identity was gone. The character I had defined and built for fifty years was conquered and broken. My safety was in a pill bottle and a zombie state. Everything around me was a threat. I was in a permanent flight mode, numb but terrified.

We did not speak in the car. I stared out of the window, feeling the heaviness of perceived judgment. I arrived home and immediately sought refuge under my weighted blanket and tried to break the rumination with the ease of daytime TV. I felt like I was crawling out of my skin. On one hand, I did not want to be around anyone, but

I was also completely terrified of being alone with my broken self. I reduced my life to surviving each second—onto the next. All I could tell myself was *Fight!* This is a place way past loneliness. It's hanging on by the fingernails to your sanity and having a real feeling that you are losing the battle. My insides were quite simply melting in a marinade of pure terror and self-loathing. Right then, I really felt like I was not going to make it, the strongest emotion I have ever felt and believed. Time for some more lorazepam.

Let me give you some insight at this point to understand what I was yet to discover as I lay there. I was raised by a generation that was the progeny of survivors of the Second World War; this mixed with the straight-backed pragmatism of the British. This was the generation that preached to boys to toughen up and really kill any emotion. I was taught from a very young age that the only characteristic that was worth anything was strength, or at least the importance of the appearance of it. I went to schools that whipped us boys with bamboo sticks as a means of adjustment. We would compare the red-purple welts in the rest rooms, but above all else, we cultivated our armor of bravado. You could never show weakness or fear among your peers, an exhibition of the alpha kind of persona. Your place in the pack was measured by your strength.

I worked out really quickly that the way to escape any kind of ridicule was to exude a strong impervious aura. My other go-to in that pack mentality was humor. This created persona was what I took into life and held onto, all at the expense of feeling. Truth is, any kind of emotion was seen by me as complete weakness. So I shut my own emotions. I mean, I do remember getting a slight lump in my throat when E.T. went home, but I did that in private.

While I did not know it yet, these experiences were the ingredients that I used to create my story, my definition, my identity. All of us do this. We build our personality, our public face out of our own imprint, and we create facts out of opinion because it is all really just an interpretation. There are no real answers, only stories and mechanisms that we choose to navigate our journey.

So now as I lay there on the floor, my insides melting in emotional turmoil, my strong-man act desolate and beyond confused,

I was lost. I had not developed the tools needed to combat such an emotional breakdown. But in all of that, I will give credit to the one little remaining vestige of that makeup. It was that part of me that gave the whisper of fight, and thank goodness for this little light because it gave me a glimmer of a chance at hope. This is where the reduction of life into moments is really the ultimate tool of survival—at least for me it was. It gave me a mathematical solution. If I had one part resolve and one part just having to get through one moment at a time, then I could crawl out of this. The how and the why would have to come later.

So right there in my isolation, life was reduced to milliseconds: just keep going, and each of those snippets I conquered, I grew a little stronger. Marginal gains were my way out. In all of this, I felt that I also had to keep appearances up. I did not want my son to see this shell of me, and I still had to partake in the function of life—bring home the bacon, as it were. The thought of this parade just shot up my anxiety even more. I was barely clinging on. How would I be able to pull off such a parade! Thankfully, it felt like it was at this moment that my angel walked into the room. "Hi, babe, I am here. You are safe. Let's get you some help." This was the most beautiful thing that could have been said to me at the time, but also the most shame provoking! To oscillate between these two worlds, hope and shame, is something that you can only really know if experienced. It completely pulls your rudder off kilter. Don't forget the ruminating thoughts that had put me in this place were all around me, damaging and hurting my family, and here my savior was: that very family.

This pickled me in such terrifying confusion. I was starting to believe I was that danger. These thoughts were just utterly relentless, so on the one hand, I wanted to run away from my family and put as much safe distance as I could between us, but then needed to cling to them as my only lifeline. I don't even think the most talented of writers can articulate how this feels. I certainly can't. All I can say is think about the most hair-raising terror that you have ever felt and then multiply that by ten—that's how it felt to me.

The worst of these times were at night in the quiet hours: my wife restful next to me, and me ashamed and disgusted how could I

9

even think these things, so now you just add sleep deprivation into the pickle juice that is your self-definition. This mix is a circle of hopelessness in those dark moments that can just eat you alive, but for that voice that you are clinging onto, keep fighting. The sun would rise and I would pull myself together. Just one more second, then I would jump on Zoom calls or drive my two-hour commute and pull off my Oscar-winning performance. In the meantime, my angel sprang into action, and the journey to redemption began.

Chapter 3

Help...Kinda

We as a society are really only grappling with mental health now. There are some courageous souls that have been prepared to tell their story in all of its starkness. We have had high-profile people come out and speak to their own battles, which is starting to make the entire issue just that little more approachable, but in my experience, we have a long way to go. I am telling my own story in the hope that it may act as an accelerator past the judgment and the feelings of shame that come with even the smallest experience of perceived stigma. I am not writing this from the vantage point of self-help, but rather just trying to give an honest account of my story and my path to redefinition. My ultimate dream is that this can give the average layperson hope that I can be relatable, and not write from a place of celebrity or cure. So all that being said, I am not making any kind of negative judgment in a general sense of the system, but just speaking to what I myself went through.

Before I could blink, I was on the way to seeing a psychiatrist. For a guy who barely even goes to the doctor, this was pretty nerve-wracking. My wife was there by my side which made it all a little easier to face. I was like jelly at this point: just wobbling to wherever I needed to go, just hoping that someone or something could help. I needed a good tonic of hope and so trusted the professionals. Besides, I had heard before about the concept of a chemical imbalance and how this was the predominant cause of these kinds of mental health episodes. So I was clinging onto the thought that there was some kind of medicine that would just take this all away. That was the narrative screaming in my psyche as I walked into the clean-cut office. I ran for the seat while my wife handled all of the front-facing process stuff. I was just not able to handle any of the normality.

I sat there, bathing in what I thought was a stigmatized scrutiny. Everybody had to know that I was here for a broken brain, this broken self-consciousness spiking my innards and requiring all the courage I had. As my wife joined me, I squeaked out, "Please come in there with me," feeling that familiar complex mix of shame and relief at having her there. I had always prided myself on being strong for her and our family, and now I had the neediness of a four-year-old, a shell of myself whimpering my way through life. That feeling of having your entire makeup up for grabs was for me the darkest place, and I wanted a fix—an easy one!

"Nicholas." The nurse was ready to start the journey. I clung onto my angel and felt the nurse quizzically respond to both of us coming into the inner chambers of hope. Mercifully, she rolled with it, and we were through. My vitals were taken in a blur. I focused on a spot on the floor, gulping. They were going to fix me—just go with it. The irony of my physical self being given a resounding bill of health was not lost on me, and truthfully, I would have taken a physical ailment in that moment in a heartbeat, but I was there to fix my head, my chemicals! Just a little longer and I would be in the comforting arms of the medical miracles of our time. I would get a magic pill and *poof*, I would be me again. We were ushered into another sun-drenched room, stark and clinical. "The doctor will be with you shortly."

We waited for what to me seemed like an eternity—come on, solution, let's go. I want out of this prison. Then there was a quiet knock on the door, and a small Asian man entered with a notebook in hand and a courteous calm demeanor. In that moment, his whole aura calmed me: here is wisdom, here is cure, my own Mr. Miyagi. I felt a warm comfort right then, which disappeared fairly quickly when he curtly asked his first question. "Why are both of you here?" the freakish terror of that question delivered like an abrasive head-master and sent me on an inward tailspin.

Please don't make her leave. I managed to blurt out something like "I need her here." He reluctantly seemed to allow this, even though it felt to me like he thought this highly irregular. But none-theless, he was my miracle worker, making me quick to forgive any of my gut tellings. He sat deliberately, totally unaware of the bated breath and pressure of that moment for me.

What followed was a litany of questions that felt like a tem-plate, a rehearsed checklist. I dug deep and answered as openly and as honestly as I could muster. At one point, even making the begging plea of "Please just make these thoughts go away." I told him that I probably had more lorazepam in my bloodstream than blood at that time, to which his head gravely shook while telling me of the devilish addictive qualities of that little white pill that was clinging me to my sanity. He took feverish notes in a tried and tested notepad before looking up and sweepingly announcing that he had a diagnosis for me!

"You are afflicted with extreme panic disorder, and I prescribe you fifty milligrams of Zoloft." *Boom*—there it was: my savior, my medicine. *I am cured*; my inner voice jumped with glee. That is until he said, "Take one tablet a day, and you will begin to feel the results in six to eight weeks." I mean, had I just heard that right? It takes six to eight weeks to fix my chemicals, and we have landed on Mars! This does not do what it says on the box. All of this struggle today, and I leave with my despair doubled. This is wrong—it just cannot be. I sometimes did not feel like I could make it through a day, let alone six weeks.

Let me unpack this because my grand hope is that my experi-ence—and the fact that I can somewhat write it down and the out-side chance of it being read and maybe some kind of analysis and/or discourse—may result in us looking at the process of this all. We need to change the way mental health is dealt with. Look aside from the stigma attached to mental health issues which I will go into a little later. We have a system, a process of treatment that is available to people struggling with something like this, and sure, I do not want to generalize, so I will just speak to what I went through.

Wrongly or rightly, I had pinned my entire hope on the fact that someone out there in the professional realm knew how to fix me, just like going to a doctor. It's important to understand the breakdown of mental definition is the most desperate of places to land yourself. All you want is someone to give you hope. I found hope in the fact that all I needed was my brain chemicals balancing, which is just a horrible narrative to place your life in. Honestly, even if it was a placebo, I did not care. I just wanted someone to say, "It's all going to be okay." This was never once communicated to me. The entire process was clinical, totally void of compassion, which had the complete opposite effect of hope. Just think about how the desperation is intensified when even the professionals seem not to care, and at worst, almost engage in the stigma. In that moment, don't sell a drug. Just tell those you diagnose that there is hope and you are there to help. That right there goes way further than making your prescription quota for big pharma.

So as we left that day, I was armed with a slow release prescription and a bigger despair.

Chapter 4

You Are on Your Own

I sat in the car, sullen, going between seeking and plunging, my miracle gone, and with it, the one real ingredient I really needed: just to be told that there was hope. I cannot explain the feeling of hopelessness when you are never told, "We have seen this before. We can help, rest assured." Right then I felt that I was afflicted with something brand-new, like some mental virus variant that the world had never seen alone. Pamela tried her best to console me. It's hard to console the hopeless. We marched off to get my prescription anyway, the six weeks looming. I felt the rising of dread clinging on for that amount of time. I seemed beyond desperate, that irrational voice whispering, "Go on, give up." I resorted to the only tool of survival I had at this time one second at a time, back to the street fight.

The one spark of real insight that I had at this time came about because I still had to partake in life. I had to work. So I decided that I would be totally vulnerable and honest with my boss on what I had been through—no sugar coating. This openness was to become my theme. I had at least made the decision that I had nothing to be ashamed about—publicly anyway. Inside was a different thing altogether. The talking about it was sowing the small seeds of catharsis. This did, however, demonstrate how we as a community find it hard to deal with the mental health prevalence. My boss, in an attempt to appear helpful, allowed me to commute less and then changed my title. So on the one hand, I got a little release from my four-hour commute, but then he made me feel like for some reason I could not fulfill my title obligations, but the demands never changed. The rumination then became that he deep down thought that I was faulty, broken, which again just intensified the feeling of stigma. The message I heard was *You are on your own.*

So what to do? I turned to the next societal solution for my position and decided to open myself to the idea of therapy. This did not come easy to me. I had spent fifty years vilifying therapy. I, in my narrow-mindedness, had deemed it indulgent and weak. But with gentle nudging from my wife we began the search for a therapist. Sadly, what transpired, to me anyway, was another example of a broken system. Therapy is expensive. Most American families are not able to add this kind of cost into their paycheck-to-paycheck existence, which by default has made the offering somewhat elitist. As an aside, all of this was happening to me deep in the jaws of the pandemic, so financial survival was front and central. This meant that my choice of therapist was really going to be driven by the appetite of my wallet. Again, I want to state that this is my experience and is not an overall judgment of therapists on the lower-hourly-rate end of the spectrum.

We found a lady close to us that offered a service that I felt like we could manage, even if it was just to see if it was something that would help. I made the call and set up the appointment. It was a week out, but at least it served as a beacon in the distance, an effort at treatment, an action which gave me a little hit of hope. These hope hits had become my version of crack cocaine: each step forward, toward which I inwardly congratulated myself, each day surviving. I breathed in that hope.

I arrived early and sat in my truck, scoping out the building, getting my bearings, and trying my best to evoke the courage needed. My body was so depleted at this point. Flight mode was hard to sustain for such a long period of time. My courage reserves were being depleted with each attempt at normalcy. I tried breathing deep, and if I am honest, the thought crossed my mind to drive out of that parking lot and just tell my wife that I had tried it and it was not for me. But giving up like that, I knew, would instinctively plunge me further into this thing that was consuming me, and besides, I needed that hit of hope, and the possibility existed of a huge hit up in that building. More guarded this time, not getting my hopes up of a miracle, I walked up the staircase, down a long passageway, and then was buzzed into another intensely brightly lit clinical room. She was just finishing up her previous appointment. I announced myself and sat in the waiting room, stewing in stigma.

She led me into her office. The proverbial couch was front and center. I had that instant dilemma: do I lie down? I sat. She introduced herself, giving me a brief introduction into who she was. Turned out that she had a full-time day job and did this therapy gig at night. I was once again immediately struck by the complete lack of compassion in her delivery: clinical. All I wanted was a hope hug, but this was simply transactional. I paid her and then she embarked on her disclaimer: because of my son at home, what I heard was anything you say can and will be used against you. My thoughts were all around my family, so really in that moment, I felt like I could not speak my truth, for fear of welfare coming around my house. We meandered through the session, me being surface and her being bored and trying to get her last appointment for the night out of there. Look, I obviously agree that minors need protection, but this whole thing was devoid of compassion and common sense, so once again, I was at a dead end. I sat in my truck, the sober thought of really being on my own in this thing screaming inside.

I had no answers. I had tried all of what the mental marketplace had to offer, and the results had been nothing short of devastating. Time to think out of the pod.

Chapter 5

Podcasts

For some relativity here, there were two fundamental struggles going on for me here. The most harrowing of the two was that I was believing these ceaseless thoughts going on, which made me a bad man by my reckoning. The second was that I was still so deeply entrenched in the brand of manhood that I had cultivated over fifty years. At this point, the idea that that was toxic was not even on my radar. So here I stood, truly believing that I was a bad man for having these thoughts, but then also ridiculing myself as being the very definition of a weakling, so this was like shame squared and an endless loop, and I just did not have the tools to even begin to come to terms with this. The only thing I could do was go inward and begin to make some changes, clinging onto the idea of doing something new in order to get a different result. All I can say is thank goodness for living in a world where there are resources available instantly and where there are more and more brave souls out there speaking their truth because it was here in this digital landscape that I had the first feelings of not being alone.

So with the two traditional pathways having left me bereft of any real solution, I needed to pivot and go deeper. I had to understand where these thoughts were coming from and why. I had slowly begun to develop the skill of at least getting through the day, mainly just knowing that I had the fight. This gave me some space to slowly reflect, and I struck upon an observation. Before all of this, I had been somewhat content. We had just bought our dream home, which was a goal a long time in the making. It did, however, come at the expense of a commute for me, which was traffic dependent. The round trip could range from three to six hours. My boss had not really grasped the concept of remote or hybrid working hours, so he was insistent that I make this trip five times a week. This meant getting up at four in the morning and often returning after seven in the evening. It was grueling, to say the least, and gave me an acute insight into the effects of sleep deprivation.

In order to make these trips bearable, I had taken to listening to podcasts. My chosen genre and the only genre was true crime. I voraciously devoured every true crime podcast I could get my ears on to and from work. I listened to the most gruesome, heartbreaking, and graphic podcasts for a minimum of three hours a day! Just peppering my conscious and subconscious mind with this disturbing imagery—I mean, it could be said that I had put in enough time to have my thesis in the worst of human nature. I loved my truck time in the dark hours before the sun came up, delving into the psychology of this side of society. Never once did I think this was an issue. In fact, quite the contrary, it was my me time.

But now in my crumpled state, I started to make the connection. This damaging cocktail of sleep deprivation and this wicked narrative just on a loop, I wondered if this could have been a contributing factor to my ruminating thoughts and the visions of self-harm and harm in general that had all of a sudden made their acquaintance. Had the universe delivered me a waking slap in the form of a cruel breakdown as a warning or a wake-up call to reevaluate my choices? My thoughts and visions were very often dream-like and disturbing, as if I had somehow flooded and poisoned my subconscious mind. I have to say I had not really connected the dots right then, but something was stirring: a curiosity, which gave me a starting point and a drip of hope. The old business adage I had heard around data: *garbage in, garbage out* seemed to apply, or at least that was my wish.

I made the call to change my subject material and decided to flood my being with enlightenment and good things, just to see if I could reverse the junk food diet of true crime. I typed in personal development in the search bar and listened to anything, praying that this was the tonic for my condition. This had two immediate effects: the first being that I was taking action. No matter how small, I was taking a step forward, marching toward change. This gave me strength. The second and most profound is that I found a digital community, a support group which made me feel that I was not alone. In fact, I found that almost everyone is going through something.

I listened to everyone from Gabby Bernstein to Steven Barlett and everything in between: personal testimonies of having been through a similar struggle. The tightness in my throat lessened slightly and I could squeak out a breath. Knowledge gathering, I allowed it to happen organically. Each one would lead me down a new rabbit hole. I was now daily engaging in epiphanies, as opposed to depravity.

I did not feel alone anymore, but at this point, all of this was just theoretical. It for sure gave me some solace, but it was mostly a narrative from people who were speaking of recovery, of being in a place where their struggle was way further in the past. These were people who were ahead of me in their becoming. I was deep in my destruction. I needed something practical, something scientific, a remedy, or at least an action that would be me progressing. This came in the form of a little intriguing nugget that I had never heard before.

I heard about the concept of neuroplasticity! It is actually fairly complicated, but Dr. Caroline Leaf put it in layman's terms for me. Essentially, she said our brain is flexible, elastic, and is grown by our thoughts, which meant with some practice, you could change your brain and control the direction of your thoughts. She said that you could kill certain established brain trees and form new ones in the image you wanted. I could redirect my intrusive thoughts, and even better yet, stop watering them, and over time, that tree would die, and you could replace it with your own manufactured tree of hope. This was not a click-of-the-fingers solution. It would require consistent work and new habit forming, but it was science-based and indisputable, and better yet, the good doctor had created an app to walk me along this process day by day.

This was a pint of hope for me, something tangible. All I needed to do was work consistently every day. At that point, I was ready to do anything. So began my journey toward something. I had no idea of the transformation ahead, but this was forward, and that in itself in that moment was enough.

Chapter 6

Neurocycle

Looking back, these were the first moments of me discovering how everything we think is interpretive. I was beginning to understand that really it is all just a contrived story, a confused soup of how we interpret all of the imprints we have been subjected to along the way. I had trusted my thoughts blindly, and they had led me to lead a story based on what can politely be described as non-facts, but more directly as lies that we tell ourselves. The seeds were beginning for me to discover the ultimate liberation of controlling and questioning all thoughts through an absolute lens of suspicion! Profound indeed, but I am getting ahead of myself here.

I arrived home that night and furiously found and downloaded the app. Of course, I had a mixture of caution and excitement. This felt right, or at least plausible. Here was a very esteemed person in her field, taking the science and making it digestible for me, simplifying it, and it made sense. At the same time though, I had been through the ringer of potential solutions and was already guarding my response to these things. Even though this was a digital process, it was steeped in compassion. Her voice was soothing and the pace of your own. The next thirty days, I was to engage in what was called a neurocycle. I would check in daily and have Dr. Leaf personally walk me through the growing of new brain trees.

Let me just say: as groundbreaking as this felt, it was also wrought with terror. It was like going into the jaws of my breakdown. I was going to have to look at it dead in the eye, be vulnerable, be honest. This was the biggest trigger I could put myself through. It was a good thing that I had been developing my fight muscle.

It started with stating and defining my intrusive thoughts. We were going to work on just one thought, so I needed to really give it a life, write it on paper, marinade in it, give it a life in order to redefine it, and eventually render it drought-stricken. To write this down was terrifying. There it was in words on paper, my shameful thought: *you are damaging and hurting your family.* My throat tightened once again. The most debilitating of emotions surging through my veins: shame with a healthy seasoning of disgust. Day one done, *gulp!* Even though this was so hard and left me in a triggered state, there was another odd feeling that began taking root. I had named my enemy, which in itself was a liberation because before this, I had kept it deep inside, bombarding my mind with hair-raising terror, but bound in secrecy. Now even though it was only for my reading, it was out on a page. It was declared and I felt emboldened, a conquering whistleblower. I see you. Now that my enemy was known and expressed, my fight tendon just wanted to give it the middle finger, and this work promised to deliver me from its debilitating clutches one step forward, but this step felt like it had meaning, it had substance. Courage is grown by staring a fear in the eye and standing firm.

What followed was a guided journey inward, an epic *Lord of the Rings* in scale, little by little each day probing and prodding deeper. The cadence was wrapped in forgiveness. I could stop at any given time but needed to come to this place daily and explore. What really resonated with me was that this process had a scientific thread, delivered by a doctor that was highly recognized in her field, but it was delivered in bite-sized chunks. In layman's terms, quite simply it was approachable. A perfect start point to the work that I would need to put in to change, to unself and rise to being a new person. I needed to do the work, but the message I received in that moment of darkness was you can change, your tree of dread and panic can die and diminish, and that I could actually grow a new mentality tree. My side of the bargain was to consistently show up, be present, and most of all, listen.

I needed to build up the skills of really listening and understanding how our brains work. It was totally uncomfortable, but honestly, I was all in. This was my pool of hope, while I still waited for the meds to kick in! This was a roller coaster, delivering me both sobering and mind-jumping epiphanies daily that I would go and reflect on, all the while fighting down the shame, living in this heightened state of fear. Would there be another episode or a tremor? I made sure that I had my "just in case" bottle of lorazepam with me everywhere I went. I continued to commute, wallowing in the feeling that I was changed, broken—just keep fighting. Some of those days were just a white-knuckle ride to just keep it together, but each day survived, meaning that I could do the next one. This daily grapple was my measurement and my only reason.

What the neurocycle process had started though was a knowledge quest, a catalyst toward just inhaling anything I could. My podcast menu totally changed. I was arming myself with the voices of our time on this subject. I listened to everything, filling myself with concepts, like a massive three-thousand-piece jigsaw scattered across my insides, in a confused, excited, and fearful stew of something. Even though I had not started the putting together of the pieces I was acting, and acting was movement, and movement meant I was not stuck or stationary, I was seeking forward and that was my tonic of survival.

Each day there were little nuggets that would give me a surge of something that was intoxicating as well as in some ways frightful—as if there was a battle royal going on inside, my identity clinging on and fighting for its existence, while the other part was pulling me toward change. Did I know what kind of change would be required at that time? Not even close, but there was a small whisper sending a rattle in my instincts. An entire overhaul of everything I had ever constructed as to who I am was about to be demolished, and one day I would have a thing to refer to as my old self. Not that I knew any of that, but that inkling was enough: just keep doing this stuff because something is happening. I know now that I was beginning a relationship with my intuition. I did not have the skills yet to understand this courting, but the whispers were there.

Chapter 7

No More Fight

Now at this moment, there was a seismic shift taking place that was beginning to shake my entire concept of what being a man is all about. But to redefine something that you have relied on for your entire life is nothing short of harrowing. To really begin to face the idea that you have been wrong or complacent all of this time is totally crushing. In order to go forward to climb out of the crisis, I needed to go back to the beginning to unravel this well-meaning, but faulted storyteller. There were so many new characteristics that I would need to truly embrace to even embark on this journey. I needed to put things in my backpack that I had previously thought of as weakness, and even worse, wimpiness. *Gulp*. Honestly, this is why my idea of the universe having delivered me a brutal reality check began to change into me perceiving it as more a reality check wrapped in compassion, but it needed to be stark so that I would take notice. Onward!

The first major shift came at what I perceived to be at a huge cost, and it would require that I abandon a part of my self-identity. That was really the main makeup of my idea of who I was. I mean really understand this: for fifty years, I had presented a persona to the world, a totally contrived character, a story. Polished and embellished along the way so that I could live with myself and be okay with my appearance to the world. It started innocently enough, but the implications were huge, and I see now was the rocket fuel to my trajectory.

At this point, I was starting to get a quiet sense of pride: one because I was just swimming through this tsunami of information, but also clinging onto my fight, my resolve. At the very heart of whom I had tried to give to the world was a guy who never gave up. I grew up playing every sport I could. I played rugby into my twenties, and more often than not, I was the smallest on the field, but I was always spoken of as having the most heart, never giving up. This recognition cemented my place in the pack, and I had used it to navigate the brutality of the playground, the quagmire of adolescence, and then into my military service, having been a conscript in the South African system. This strength, or even the outward perception of it, had been my ticket to being accepted. So whether consciously or subconsciously, I had chosen to ride this train no matter what. This was "me." I attacked everything in life from the standpoint that I could not be broken.

Every aspect of my life was peppered with this foundation: breakups, business failings, and standing right next to my boys in any situations that may arise out there. I started without ever being conscious of this, really spraying my entire life with this one thing. I was strong and in so many ways emotionless. A one-trick pony, I had a one-size-fits-all methodology to anything that life threw at me and I clung to it with varying results, but it was whom I saw in the mirror. I was a survivor, plain and simple.

So clearly on the day that I had life deliver me a breakdown. I reverted to type and took pride in my fight. In fact, it was the reason why I felt I was alive. But nothing was changing. Each morning I would wake up and brace myself against the rumination, put up my dukes, and fight. This insistent brawl—was this my new life? That thought right there always brought terror because in this case, I was not sure of how long I could put up this fight. This was an inward foe, one that I did not understand, a master grappler that had me in a chokehold, and time was running out. The feeling of empty hopelessness when you know you're goto is out of its depth and you have nothing else in your arsenal is just simply terrifying. I would toss and turn in the quiet dark hours of night in this grapple and wake each day answerless, and revert to type, the emotional exhaustion on a ticking clock like a doom shadow ever present.

Then my good neurocycle doctor introduced me to an idea. It came in the form of almost a throwaway comment, a cliché of these circles. Initially I did not know what to make of it, but as she provided more perspective, more meat on this kernel, I felt a tingle. My throat was weirdly clogged and open at the same time. "What resists, persists." In of itself this had a kind of public speaking ring to it until she literally personalized it to my exact situation. The more you fight that intrusive thought, the more it persists. I mean, talk about a crushing liberation. In one grand sweep, she had given me both a chance at freedom, but also taken away the only tool I had at my disposal.

I was throwing gasoline on my rumination, and yes, believe me, it was definitely persisting. But the thought of losing that part of my built character meant that I would have to question everything. All that had carefully constructed and sculptured, all that I had been to the world was in question. It hit me right between the eyes. In this case, the worst thing I could do was fight! But man, what was the alternative? I had nothing, then she introduced the antidote. She delivered one word, a word that came so loaded, it threw my insides into a mash of emotions. It echoed through me like a shattering of everything I stood for.

Chapter 8

Surrender

Let me give this some reference because the last thing I would want anyone to think is that I am being flippant and making out if any of this is or was easy. This is a continuous look deep inside, which is filled with foreign concepts, that really stretched and confused. And the biggest of all, they challenge the status quo of everything you have ever known to be true. This is the place where growth happens. Nothing grows in comfort. It makes our spirit lazy. We accept things the way they are. As cliché as it is, the only way to deeper insight is to jump into the arms of challenge and embrace growth. It also needs to be said that I was winging it for the most part. I had no road map out of this. I just went where the journey took me, armed myself with as much knowledge as I could, and then just rolled with it.

So surrender. I mean, this was probably the most foreign of ideas that I could be presented with, given that my entire construction had been around strength. Every life event that I ever went through was met with resolve, resilience, and doggedness. As I said before, this was my one-size-fits-all method. I had wrapped my entire nobility around the fact that I could hang on by the fingertips and celebrate my one-dimensional power. I saw this as my competitive advantage. I had not even contemplated that there was another way, and I had done this for the better part of fifty years. What was required to even embrace this concept was a complete unraveling of everything I had thought to be true. The first step into pulling on this life-changing thread was to understand surrender and then jump into its abyss with complete trust.

How does one understand something like this without being overwhelmed? I decided to take it slow one step at a time: just let the idea reverberate through my core, and I asked the universe to guide me through this unknown. Had I been wrong all of this time? Was it possible that vulnerability could actually be a kind of strength, and even better yet the good kind? All I needed for these ideas to begin stewing was to be open to the possibility, but my fifty-year legacy was fighting hard, stubborn in its rightness. This tussle right in the midst of a life crisis, which for me felt like all I had was fight—how could I let that go? I mean, it felt like on top of what I had been through, I was now being led to a place of questioning everything I was. This added just another layer of terror. Scary contemplation. I needed something to unlock all of this, then I had a conversation with someone whose opinion I respected, which gave me a chance to jump.

Let me say for starters: a choice I made that held me in good stead and allowed for this unlocking conversation was I had decided to speak openly about what I was going through, naked, exactly my experience. Not only did this allow me to know that others were having their struggles, but it invited other perspectives into my con-sciousness—thought bombs that sent me in a confused spiral, but in the background, there was this little knowing telling me faintly that this was a worthy rabbit hole. Be brave.

I had opened up to a friend and told him exactly what I had gone through. He had finished my sentences, saying things like, "And then your suicidal thoughts, and the panic grew."

I was gobsmacked with his intimate knowledge of it. Turns out that he had been through something uncannily similar. I was waxing lyrical about this surrender thing. Almost mocking it in my well-versed bravado when he said, "Once you surrender, you begin your journey of rebirth. When you stay in resistance, you remain in fear. Let it go, bro." A rebirth? WTF. It sounded like utopia, but what did it mean? I was okay. I had made it this far, now I needed to be reborn?

But there was that little voice inside the new one, whispering, "He is right." Work it out; dig deep. The beginning of this journey begins with surrender.

Chapter 9

I Have Been Wrong
All This Time!

The idea of a rebirth is both liberating, but also chastising. I, for so long, really preached and believed that I was one of the good guys. I held onto concepts like integrity, honor, chivalry—all of the societal ingredients that I thought the world wanted to hear. But I was also emotionally closed, my insides as stiff as a block of protective marble. I could not feel, but I was well versed in the act of feelings, so I could get by on the face of it, but was always exposed when intimacy called. So for this part of the journey to begin, I had to start to learn how to feel again because after all, the good Dr. Leaf had said, "There is no healing without feeling." Double gulp.

As that door opened, it was as if there was a new voice inside—a wiser one as I opened up and accepted where I was at and let go of the self-judgment and began to accept it without opinion. Slowly, some answers started to form. It started with me reframing the thoughts that I had. I had to make them a little more digestible, acceptable, which then allowed for a deeper scrutiny that was with less fear. I reframed these thoughts by seeing them as a metaphor, just like the subconscious mind can often give us completely wacky dreams, visually vivid. Maybe this was how I was being communicated to, and because I had not heeded previous signals, the universe had decided I needed something direct in my face to really get the point across.

This put some distance between me and those thoughts, which started me on the stark realization that I was not my thoughts, like whoa, we are not our thoughts? Who knew! This seemingly small idea absolutely rocked my core because if I am honest, my thoughts and my reaction to them had pretty much dragged me around by my nostrils for my entire life. My ceaseless internal dialogue had sculpted my persona, the way I saw myself, and the way I wanted the world to see me. But it was all based on opinion, legacy, and all of the social measurements that we are plagued by. I was crafted by the outside environment, made to conform or please. I have chased all of the man-made badges of honor, cars, houses, and appearances because my thoughts had driven me to be seen a certain way, this mad task-master pushing all of the buttons, creating falsity and disharmony inside. The chemical trail being blazed across my insides, stress being my proud anthem, the scarcity mindset pushing me further away from myself, and never being enough.

What was even harder to swallow was that I had chased all of this with a smug disposition—my ego, the gasoline. I am better because my aura was percolating in judgment, living in the future, trying to demolish the Joneses. Now here I was faced with an epic crisis that had brought real meaning into my life, a shooting star of clarity and of priority. I sat and pondered the fact that I have been wrong all this time. What has my slavery to my inner voice driven me to covet, and what expense and why had the universe deemed it necessary to slap me so hard to wake me up? Was I so out of touch with my inner self that I was brought to the edge of driving my truck off a cliff when I seemingly had everything? This deep discomfort churned my insides, making me feel things. It felt like a thread on a woolen jacket that once I gave it a tug, it would just unravel, and I would be someone else on the other side.

This created this weird mixture of anxiety and excitement in the bottom of my stomach. The fear was always there, but now with this becoming, this journey inward, I was excited because it felt like the light and the end of the tunnel. This cosmic riddle, once I worked it out, was going to be a liberation like nothing else. I would find my untrustworthy thoughts running wild into where this is going? This struggle, this discovery, terrified me then, jumping out of my skin with a feeling. Just keep going, surrender to the process, and all will be revealed. One thing that I had decided concretely was that this was a warning. You have to stop, take a breath, and reexamine here. Something had to change—of that I had become certain.

The great riddle: all I could do was create a safe place to look at the message. These wicked thoughts—what were they trying to tell me? This was in so many ways the hardest thing I have ever done in my life because even though I had been able through the reframing process to actually look at these thoughts and write them down even, they were dripping in shame for me. For me, this sludge of shame that I was living at this time was at times completely unbearable, but there was something different inside me. My courage was now wrapped in vulnerability. I now saw emotion as strength, and so was able to ride this wave of disgust, feel it out, and over time realize that it was not me.

With this acceptance, I started to make headway with the riddle, *what are you trying to tell me?* If these thoughts had been around my family, then that was where I had to start, not knowing at the time what this was going to unlock, but that light in the distance had just got a little brighter.

Chapter 10

Dad

I had given up on the fatherhood process in my life. I was most definitely a confirmed bachelor. I suppose this was a mixture of failed relationships, and mostly a huge fear of being responsible for others. I know now that any time a relationship got close to this social idea of station wagons and picket fences, I would slowly sabotage and extricate. I found comfort or reprieve in flying solo and had built my entire worth around work. Being the first to arrive and the last to leave gave me this sense of nobility. I had somehow bucked the social prescription. I could play Xbox, drink beers on weekend mornings, and work myself to the bone all in the name of freedom. I would smirk inwardly as another one of my mates succumbed to the ball and chain of matrimony. That was my thinking anyway.

But the longer I got into that, there was a growing sense of meaninglessness, no legacy. My work endeavors were no longer giving me any real satisfaction. It was the hamster wheel slog. A barren landscape of no appreciation and sadly, a dearth of piss-poor leaders in the workspace, in my opinion. Even with this growing feeling, I still felt like the dad train had left the station, which I had created a sort of ambivalence about. There was this deep sense of incongruence because I was having recurring thoughts of legacy. Sitting in the bleachers of all of my friends having kids and seeing the profound changes in them that this had brought about just fueled this. Kids are legacy in many ways, and I had, it seemed, willfully pushed this natural cycle away—for what? Just to create material wealth for others. It had begun to look like a poor decision on my part. Especially since my high standards of what I thought success to be, I had not met.

The universe did, however, have other plans, and thankfully so. All I needed to do was make a leap of faith. This came in the form of an online dating app and matching with my person, and *boom*, the universe brought a wonderful lady into my life, and she had a little three-year-old redhead bundle of energy, and yes, Legacy. We were married, and I was Dad. This role, it turned out, was at the center of this huge soul search that I now found myself in. It was to take me on a profound journey inward that would have me go back in order to go forward. I am going to leave this chapter here, and then come back to how it all tied in, just to say that there is nothing like being a parent that brings the way you were parented into sharp focus, warts and all.

Chapter 11

Roots

My family and I have immigrated three times in our lives. Let that sink in; that means leaving your home to a new country and culture. Even though the world is a global village, immigration is tough. Each time we did it as a family was in pursuit of a better, more secure life, fleeing the instability and propensity for war on the African continent. I mention this only because when I had made the connection that I would need to unravel my molding and the impact my created story has had on my life, this starting again requires resolve and resilience. It's kinda no wonder I had adopted those characteristics as my priorities.

I was the only member of my family that was born in Africa, a far-flung colony called Rhodesia. My mom and blood father had rather courageously sought out something there. My parents had both, I suppose, different reasons for fleeing the North of England to the sun-drenched shores of my homeland. My dad was a renegade and a gambler by nature and probably believed that there was a fortune to be found in the colonies. My mom was escaping the dogma of a militant Roman Catholic household, having already committed the horrendous crime of being with child out of wedlock.

I never really ever got to know my blood father. He was tragically killed in a car accident, and before that, they were divorced. So when I was confronted with my own molding by my son and my newfound role as parent, I looked at my mom's journey and what made her parent the way that she did. It also needs to be said that the father figure in my life is my stepfather Philip, who is really my dad. So in order to know some of the things I began to do and implement as a parent, I had to look closely at my parents. This can be a scary process, and I was very cognizant of it not turning into some kind of witch hunt and just an examination of the warts because I believe that I had a good childhood. But the real truth at this moment was that I felt that my parenting methods were not working and in fact were damaging, hence the breakdown.

So with a torn mind, I slowly but sympathetically began to make some sense of how I was made and the stories that I had held onto, all with the new realization that it is all a construct based on perception and the adding of our own ingredients to make some sense of life. The first real observation that hit me was just how different life was for my mum—a totally different world that she lived in, so I could never really understand the choices that she made because I had no understanding of her environment. This in turn meant that all of my discoveries and opinions would be hearsay. There was no way for me to relate, but nonetheless, I continued forth.

For starters, my grandpa was a survivor of the beaches of Dunkirk in the Second World War. He came back deaf, and I can only assume broken. I could never imagine the horrors that he must have lived through. We never had a relationship, so anything that I know of him is mostly anecdotal. That in itself is very limited because as a family, we don't talk about these things. It's the British way. By all accounts, he ruled his house with an iron fist: the rod of staunch Catholicism, his justification for the punishments meted out. My mum, Moira, is the oldest of five, so my only real deduction was that she bore the brunt of most of this ire, which in turn meant that she developed a real thick skin and a calloused heart. She is also headstrong and full of spirit, which meant her natural response was rebellion and the middle finger to Grandpa. It was no doubt this renegade spirit that led her to Billy, my dad, who was himself a rebel and the cock of the North. Not exactly the kind of suitor that you want to bring home to Dad, never mind falling pregnant with his progeny. Talk about a hand grenade. What would the neighbors say!

So with all of this, my mum must have developed her own survival instincts, which was a hardening, a tough presentation to the world, and suffering in privacy and silence. In my house, love was a given, but not really a demonstration. The last thing you wanted to be was "mushy." Just imagine that social narrative that must have come out of the Second World War: Winston Churchill echoing through everything, the construct was just simply put your head down and get on with it, and indulgent emotion was just not a thing. After all, it had been this that had allowed for the saving of the world, so if it ain't broke, don't fix it. Instead, just shelf it and take a step forward. It really struck me how generationally different we were. Here I was, living in the lap of the American dream, which could not have been any different from what my mum had had to navigate. This sobering insight allowed me to view my upbringing through a lens of understanding other than judgment. While this made it a much easier reflection, I was still aware that because of how the world had moved on in terms of its sensibilities, I had to tweak my parenting. I needed to cherry-pick the good from the bad, and more importantly, be relevant to the environment that my little guy was growing up in.

Added to this was the cultural piece. I had grown up in Africa, a place drenched with the British methodology of the way children were tailored. I grew up in a time when behavior modification in the home was a smack on the bottom, and would then go into a school system that had corporal punishment as a prominent part of its disciplinary process. As I mentioned earlier, this was in the form of caning. Two of the best were the minimum and then six of the best were the maximum, and everything else in between reflected the severity of the crime. We grew into this as normal, the threat of it always there, and believe me, it worked. If you could see past the boy bravado outside that office, there was a kind of exhilarating terror as you stood outside the office, waiting for your name to be called. The worst times were when you were on your own with no accomplices to act strong for, I can remember times shivering outside the office of a one Mr. Des Fontein, who was reputed to be the hardest accurate striker. There was talk of him being able to place welt upon welt. Sadly, I had become fully entrenched on his radar, so I was able to corroborate the whispers.

All this being said, I felt like I had turned out okay, so I did not ever have any bitterness toward this ideology. Now however as a newfound dad, the world had done a complete about-turn of these things, so my frame of reference was an outdated relic. Not that I would ever partake in the strike fest, but my fathering had the tough overtones of my history, which cast me as the bad cop in my home, which had clearly manifested itself in a guilt-ridden way, so I needed to reflect and reform. But to do that, I had to go inward.

Chapter 12
Dad (2)

So even though my nights were still filled with these hair-raising crazy thoughts, I was starting to get an idea of where to look to make some sense of what it was that had tormented my spirit in such a way. I started to look at my interactions with my son and my family overall, I tried to be in each moment as opposed to being in what I had told myself my parenting philosophy was.

Things started to show themselves to me, as my spirit was saying, *remember this*! I remembered a time on a vacation in Germany where my son had left the table at a restaurant and began playing in water near some other diners. I had expressed my outrage to a table of my entire extended family. They were in turn outraged at my reaction. I stormed off in a huff which came really close to me losing my entire family unit right there, and of course, my little guy had witnessed this. The difficult part for me in that instance was that I felt completely right in my reaction. All I could revert to was how my mom would have handled the same situation with me.

Once I had opened this floodgate of examination, though I saw things with heartbreaking clarity, the moments where I would tell my son "What are you crying for?" followed up with, "You need to toughen up." My wife would then intervene, which set me off even further. After all, we needed to be a unified force. But I could see in those moments the way she looked at me. She just did not agree.

I would then shrink into the victim mentality, wax lyrical on how she was molly coddling him, and rant and rave in an attempt to get her to come over to my way of thinking, knowing deep down that I was just trying to justify my actions. This whole entire affair would result in a colossal sulk on my part, a woe-is-me mentality, and being self-alienated from both of them with bad cop stamped across my forehead.

But I stuck to my guns because I truly thought that I was doing the right thing. I mean my toughness I felt had worked out for me, and we all know that life can be hard, and the most important job I had on this planet was to prepare this little guy for life. So I was now embroiled in a difference of opinion, which divided my household and, if I am really honest, began to develop a collection of self-loathing on my part. Each time there was a situation that required a response to our son's actions. I would go plowing forward with my brand of parenting and be once again embroiled in another saga.

After time, I responded in my typical sulky way and decided to remove myself from these moments and left it to Pamela, my wife, to handle, all the while seething in the corner and judging the method. I know that my son would see my looks of disdain. We would have these moments where our eyes would meet, and he would hang his head in a sense of shame, knowing that he was somehow disappointing me. Writing this now is utterly mortifying for me. I mean, in those moments I was simply scarring his self-esteem, I see that now, but at the time, I grew colder, more distant. I think I needed to be right because the alternative was that I was hurting my family. At the time, I could not even contemplate that I was damaging the people that I loved the most. So my response was to fight to be right, all the while looking at my son in a judgmental way every time he cried. After all, I never cried. Each time he hung his head in response was like a missile to the core of my spirit, just shots that I was not prepared to acknowledge.

After a while, I believe that I was simply engaging in the process of being a parent. I was lost in history and not understanding this Dad thing. I would sit in my truck in the lonely moments of the commute and just ruminate on how no one understood where I was coming from. Nevertheless, I leaned into my stubborn nobility. Everyone else was wrong, the world was wrong; I had turned out okay, and that was all the affirmation I needed.

So each day, returning home from my commute was like an atmospheric lottery card. I never knew what state my sanctuary would be in. I just prayed for harmony so that I could pour myself a reward and retreat. All the while totally oblivious to the damage that was building inside like a boil waiting to explode. I was the minefield of eggshells that my family was trying to navigate. Even though I was initially in a deep state of denial and I was trying to justify my broken aura, there was a small knowing buried deep, and one thing was for sure: if my subconscious mind had decided to send me a message wrapped in raw brutality, I needed to heed this call.

But let me just say at this point, oftentimes when stories of these kinds of discoveries are told, they don't do the wrestle justice. I was completely resistant to any kind of admission. It was so easy for me to point the finger of blame elsewhere—nothing was my fault. I had adopted a victim mentality and I was braising myself in this slow cooker of woe is me, all the while living in this fight for survival. Something needed to happen to pull that thread and begin the unraveling. After all, I was to find—in order to rebuild I was to shatter everything—my entire view on who I was would have to change, but a fifty-year internal bunion was sure going to put up a fight. Even though I felt I was starting to understand the message, I did not know how to start the journey. It needed a spark, a sobering catalyst, which came in the form of outrage.

Chapter 13

Grumpoid

"Grumpoid needs a vacation." I heard this conspiratorial quip between my wife and my son. There it was—they had named what I was feeling inside. My initial response was all wrapped in ego, outrage, hurt, all of the blame emotions. Now it was a fact: my people had given me a nickname! Our family often wraps things in humor, so this was a normal method of messaging, but this one hit me close, right on the bone. After all of the pointless denial, I had to sit with the fact that my energy had become a living thing, a label. It was no longer this esoteric inward battle. It had a life, and it lived right in the middle of this little family unit. My family unit, and I was the protagonist, the villain in my own life.

There it was—the spark that ignited me, a starting point. If I could fix my temperament, I would be whole again. I could ride in on my white horse and claim the role of hero in my life, reclaim my place. This realization was simplistic and I was still looking for a quick fix, that imprinted pragmatism saying, "Let's just get this done and move on." I would just wake up every morning and smile and be super fun Dad—easy! I tried this contrived fakery for a while, but sooner or later, I would be triggered by something and I would feel my ire rise again, and there he was again—Mr. Grumpoid. The added wrinkle this time, however, was that we were in fact on vacation in the paradise that is Maui. I would wake up every morning with this panoramic view of the palm trees and the ocean. The promise of a relaxing cocktail in hand by the pool, and yet here I was, grumpy!

It seemed that there was no quick fix. This was not just a con job on my psyche, a fake smile. I needed to go deeper and understand why I had become this way. All of this upheaval churning inside me, a skin-crawling mystery, deeply entrenched in survival mode. Man, this was tough, and many times I felt completely hopeless. My future was now tainted. I was surrendering, fighting, doing all the things that I felt were my way out, but yet my throat was still clogged and my heart stiff. What now?

This is just an indication that the journey to self is not linear. It looks more like a graph of a seven-scale earthquake, this topsy-turvy journey of ups, downs, and everything else in between. This is the struggle of mental health because all the while this soup is mushing on the inside, we are required to appear normal in order to continue with the demands of life. As an aside here, this for me is the piece that we need to look at as a society. The fear of the stigma is so strong. To be labeled faulty in the workplace and anywhere else is deep-seated, so often it results in engaging in an illusion of fineness. The level of strength this takes is immeasurable and is totally relative to the person experiencing it. Conversations need to be encouraged and that level of transparency and vulnerability needs to be lauded as the greatest strength. These people are not broken; they are just becoming. Compassion and empathy are needed, and in my opinion, the last little healing ingredient should be admiration.

There is a certain brand of courage it takes to admit that there are things that you are doing and have been doing wrong all the time. The ego is a strong and conniving foe that masks itself in being an ally, but really, it's a poison chalice that leads us to doing things that are dominated by the self. This is only exemplified and irrational when your self is in survival mode. Let's just say that my ego was extremely healthy. While on the outside I was well skilled at presenting humility, on the inside, I thought I knew it all and would often smirk and patronize at the world around me, which ultimately killed curiosity. How could I be curious if I already knew it all? But the real truth is that being curious is one major ingredient needed to decipher this riddle. We have to second-guess our thoughts because they are laced with bias—and a predominantly negative bias at that.

When I was grumpy, it was easy for me to explain it away as being the world's fault. I would look at my family as if they had no answers. I was the oracle of wisdom, and they should just follow my lead and everything would be okay. Never once did I think that they may have a point, and really my spirit was just frustrated with me and my blindness, and it came out in a dark cloud, my aura puncturing the air around signaling disapproval and judgment. I have heard this being called a spiritual emergency, the universe having tried many things along the way to nudge me toward rethinking, taking space to look. But I, in my blind arrogance, had just plowed forward because I knew what I was doing! So really, I gave my spirit no choice but to make me take notice, and once those floodgates had opened, there was no stopping. Adapt or die because for there to be life, there needs to be growth.

I came to understand that I had been living in two major emotions: one of which had pretty much been a lifetime pursuit, and the other was the sharp end of the spear that I was being forced to swim in now. I need to write about both of these because I believe them to be the gasoline of mental health, and as a man with the trained method of burying things, I just lived with these as perennial partners, which is in itself heartbreaking, but made even more so by the fact that they are for the most part self-inflicted, as well as self-watered until they are just a sad companion. Something that I learned to live with—as do I think most men—because my generation of men are not supposed to feel or even worse show this first emotion, and ultimately, it invites the second one as a byproduct. Evil twins that feed off grumpy, blame, judgment, and kill our spirit. This is the toxic brand of manhood we created.

So let's go on a ride of releasing these two right now and set them free. Speaking to them will suck out their power because they like the shadows we give them. Time to turn on the searchlight and out these two, surrender them to exposure, and begin the road to healing and redefining.

Chapter 14

Fear

This guy—fear, my perennial companion—for me and my generation was really the barometer of our perceived manhood. The way that we handled or seemingly handled it was always present and scrutinized by the pack. Anytime it was shown outwardly was like a black mark on your scorecard, and you were always tested. Fear grew with me from the relatively small fry tests in the playground—how you stood up to bigger kids, even bullies. To the more sophisticated fears that came into adulthood, like livelihood and providing and status. Fear was always there, quietly sneering and mocking because it was mostly felt in private. This was a secret relationship, one built on dishonesty, seen when you looked in the mirror just before you put on your brave face mask as you walked out the door.

I was imprinted with a definition of manhood that was all around not ever showing weakness, standing tall. There were things that men were just not supposed to do publicly. Vulnerability was not even a concept. We were asked to navigate all of the vagaries of life with this fake machismo at the center of it, and we were constantly measured by how well we did. Man pushes buddy in a bar, tensions explode, his friends rally around your friend, and your choices are walking into that situation right next to your mate when outnumbered to a sure-fire beating, or walking away and letting your buddy down. Which was the lesser of the evils a black eye and a bloody nose, or your reputation of being scared running through your group like wildfire. In my day, this was not even a choice.

So what we did was hide our true feelings and create a dishonorable relationship. There was no honoring the struggle, only hiding from it, pushing it down, and not dealing with it. In my case, and I believe for many others, I went further and wrapped my fakery up in a warm blanket of nobility. Look at me—how strong I am by not dealing with fear, just hiding from it. So in every aspect of life, that fear reared its smirking self. I just reverted to pushing it away, faking it until I made it. Trouble is, it is one thing to stand next to your buddies in the trenches, but the nature of fear by the natural process becomes way more complicated going right to the core of how you define yourself. That's when running from this can have dire consequences because of the stone-walled insides it creates, and in some ways, everything becomes a lie.

Take the idea of providing as an example. I grew believing that a man above all else must provide. This created a new yardstick: the wonderful trappings of status. If I did not drive a flash car and have a fancy job title or a table in the back of the latest club, then I was a failure. Now I could fake the standing next to my mate in the trenches, but the obsession with status and how society still today attaches a place on the rung as a result of the ostentatious presentation of things—that's black and white, and I had a big black X on my scorecard. I bought into this fickleness hook, line, and sinker, which drove me to things like workaholism and credit card debt just to keep up with the Joneses, all the while being eaten by fear at night in private. Always fearing that I was not enough and not ever having the courage to speak to someone, a close friend about the fear because we men did not out ourselves like that. Out there I was Mike Tyson, a presentation of strength, gutted by fear of the next challenge outing me and showing the world that I, too, felt sickening fear.

But each day as I peeled myself out of bed to face another day of contrivance, I did it with pride. I lauded my own ability to not show any weakness. When I paid my staff and not myself and robbed Peter to pay Paul in my business, I felt noble I was providing. But then that night I would go to bed fearing the tax man or my landlord coming to arrest me or put me out on the street. This ever-revolving door of scarcity cloaked in nobility because after all, it's hard to live a fake. I certainly did not have the self-awareness to unpack any of it, so I just pushed on deeper, vindicated by the fact that I was fulfilling my duties as a man. But while I was portraying an outward appearance to the world of all things good, I was doing it to my own detriment, which was really just taking me further away from my spirit. I was having to make up a purpose; otherwise, the starkness of this hamster wheel would have been unbearable.

This relentless repetition of survival deadened everything. In order to do this for the length of time I did, I simply had to close major parts of my being off. I shut the door and wrapped my soul and its intuitions up in a massive chained chest. Nothing inward; my entire life was outward. Presenting this picture of a dutiful man, engaging in the societal expectations placed on my generation, never once considering that it was somewhat, if not entirely, self-inflicted.

If I am really honest, I may have never really come to a place of true examination of this construct, continued the lie, and lived with this questioning emptiness of if this was what life was. My shallow purpose of appearances and perception was my legacy. Here lies a man who believed he fulfilled his duty as a man. The only thing that made me stop in my tracks was having the great privilege of being the custodian of how my little guy would go into the world, and what toolbox I would give him. My spiritual emergency all arose from the realization that I was creating the same false sense of duty in him, placing the same silly male principles on his small shoulders. This continuance of the cycle created a bruising between us. He could feel my disappointment, and I was walking arms linked with subconscious guilt. While my liberation started with my realization that I needed to break the cycle of duty and false nobility, this old foe of fear was certainly not going to allow me such an easy escape. The next move was to invite the evil twin to the party.

Chapter 15

Shame

In my opinion, this is the tip of the spear of mental illness, the enforcer that undoubtedly has a huge part in making people jump or chug down a fistful of pills. This chapter will for sure be the hardest for me to write simply because this emotion took me to the lowest point I have ever been. I sat at its disgusting altar, ordering tankard after tankard of self-loathing, while the bartender, my thoughts, had me believing it all. This was the very issue: when you think that you are a good man—faulted, but overall good—and then your thoughts do an about-turn on you and have you truly believing that you are a bad man. This feeling of being ashamed just crushes you, nauseates each atom of your core, the walls constricting with seemingly no way out. Dark place indeed.

My lifelong identity was just peeled away abrasively like coarse sandpaper, leaving me in a place where I did not trust myself. These graphic thoughts of what a danger I was to my family and even the greater public. My throat was in constant gulp mode, swallowing down a thick tonic of fear and shame. The evil duo working seamlessly in tandem had me crawling out of my skin all the time, run! But the world around me just went on. Bills needed paying, work and family duties needed honoring, and I suffered behind a fake smile, each day hope being sucked away from me. I was lost in a perceived shameful undeserving existence all because my thoughts were out of whack, and I believed every iteration because I always had. This is the essence of mental illness. Because of the stigma we as a society have attached to this, as well as men feeling like there is no way to talk about this without being weak, we suffer these things alone. This has to change.

Without hope, there are no dreams, no goals, no happiness in many ways. In those moments, anything worth living for is gone, ripped away. Very little punctures that darkness, and I now make no judgments on decisions and actions that are taken in this dark gloom. I had people in my camp, a loving glance from my wife, a hard hug from my son—little things that signified a reason. Not everyone is this fortunate because for me, just one little shot of hope in whatever form kept me seeking. This seeking led to a little more hope. There had to be answers out there. There had to be a way out of this night.

I mentioned before that podcasts had given me a glimmer of a community that was not scared to talk about things. There I found big alpha males, tattooed to the hilt with biceps bigger than my thigh, courageously speaking of their painful journey. Each podcast fired the hope syringe, my gateway drug into the medium that I truly felt dragged me toward the brightest light, all the way to redemption and then thriving, so today, I self-identify as a lightworker. A bringer of hope, this medium, and my absolute obsession with them, dealt me in earth-shattering epiphanies that saved my sanity and life.

Chapter 16

Books

Given that I had wrongly or rightly decided that the kind of therapy that I would gravitate to was out of my wallet's reach, I had to look elsewhere for a therapeutic solution. I found this in books. As mentioned before, my main literary choice before all of this had been true crime. I was fascinated by biographies of all sorts of men who lived doing bad things. My podcast shift had started bearing fruit, so I decided to pivot the pages I chose to read as well. I did this in an organic way, and my new intuition that I was starting to hear had finally whispered, "Let the books choose you." I know that to some this may sound a little woo-woo, but as you will find in further chapters, woo-woo no longer scares me. I am a total convert.

So how did books choose me? It was quite simple. Every time—which was often—that a book was suggested on one of the podcasts I was listening to, I would scribble the title down and immediately order it on Amazon. Then I would proceed to devour it just so that I could get to the next one. Now it has to be said that I am a pretty voracious reader, but there was a deep hunger and thirst driving this newfound obsession. Pamela marveled at the speed at which I would read these bound packets of hope, but I knew innately that I had found my salvation my way out.

Let me go off on another tangent here, just to paint the landscape. During this time, my brand of manhood was really at odds with my role as Dad. I had come to this conclusion in private, and as usual, was suffering the mental debris alone. Even though to a certain degree I had identified the source, I had no tools of understanding to change. I was always aware of the stigma, so I held on so tight to my definition of man. Tough it out, but do it in silence. Cowboys don't cry: my imprinted mantra. When you suffer in silence and don't seek out outside opinion because that would entail talking about and admitting weakness, what you do is just spray fertilizer over that rampant well-meaning but crazy little voice in your head. That voice is your defense mechanism, your DEFCON system, so it lives in a world of irrational high alert. Suffering in silence is like the gasoline to panic, and before you know it, your insides are at DEFCON 5, sitting in front of that red button.

What was worse in my case—which I will hazard a guess is not uncommon among men—was that this secrecy of suffering had me believing that I was the only one ever to go through such a thing, to have the thoughts that I was having, etc. Now I knew that this could not be the case really, but I was swimming in a pot of irrationality, a panicked voice. The net result of all of this unknowing was that I was lost, which as a natural fixer was close to unlivable. But here among these hallowed pages, I found a deep community, a meat-on-the-bones community. Brave souls who were willing to speak their truths, completely and concisely.

You see, books just gave more substance to what podcasts can only really glean over. This community became my therapist's couch. I heard the heavyweight champion of the world, Tyson Fury, speaking of his day, speeding down the road toward a bridge to drive off. The ultimate alpha admitting to mental strife—talk about relatable courage. I read everything from Buddha to neuroscience. I read of survival in the Nazi death camps and comebacks from strokes. Mo Gowdat spoke of a renaissance brought on by the avoidable loss of a son. Courage and suffering were just burning off these pages. My world was beginning to open. Hope was readily available. All I needed to do was open a book.

This was my method. We each need to find our way through our suffering. For me, the messenger needs to be relatable—an everyday person going through everyday sufferings—and then be open about the deeper sufferings. I found these people in books. These dealers in epiphanies were my therapy. Each day they would sympathetically deliver a lightning bolt to my soul, the biggest thunderclap reverberating into my jelly-like innards. *You are not alone.* With each one of these, a crack of light began to pierce the darkness and begin the healing, and hope was available. The start of my comeback started with almost an obvious idea, but one that I had no idea of. But it was an agent of extreme change, a late gift from which my rising would stem.

Chapter 17

Awareness

I mentioned before that I had stumbled across the idea that our thoughts are completely unreliable. I really grappled with this because I had placed all my life bets on my thoughts. My ego had wrapped its tendrils around my inner narrative, which meant that I had smirkingly believed myself entirely for my life. I felt like I had a higher level of intelligence and was very prone to preaching to whoever would listen that I had the answers to life. I was all knowing. I would articulate the solutions to all the vagaries of life as if I was some kind of shaman, wrapped in a cloak of piety.

Even when the social measurements of life did not place me in the higher echelons of status and success—which could signal to world that I may be an imposter and in fact not have any answers—I just created an internal narrative of being a struggling artist, renouncing all of the materialistic trappings of the system. I would ignore the little murmurs in the bottom of my belly that actually desired those very trappings. I was awash in envy and judgment for those around me that had achieved this idea of success. I labelled them as shallow and chasing the wrong things. I was scathing in my private judgments, but happily drank at their VIP tables. My thoughts always had a justification, which for the most part, were always negatively skewed and judgment-based.

So as a result of all of this, I had created a somewhat pompous outlook, but unbeknownst to me was just concreting the scarcity mindset. Really, I had backed myself into a corner, I held onto my contrived story so stubbornly and was so invested in my identity that I had prohibited success, purely because of how I had convinced myself of its disdain. This for me was the self-inflicted trap of scarcity, but such was the incongruence that I still outwardly pursued the appearance of success. I dived into entrepreneurship and started my own business, which now, looking back, had no chance of success because of my minimalist mindset.

Even worse still, I encased this stiff mindset in nobility. I was doing all of this with a purer purpose, so when I did not pay myself, I felt like Ghandi. This was the fate of the struggling artist. Put simply, I wore my poverty like a badge of honor. It was poverty in all aspects, but as I have to come to find out, the highest detriment to my spirit. This survival state is a slog, maybe even an addiction. It allows you to sit in judgment of the world and swim in your woe-is-me mindset at the same time as compulsively convincing yourself of how wrong all of them are. This a revolving narrative that your thoughts gleefully put on a loop and drive you further into desolation. This is all insidious because all the while you feel like you are in charge and are in fact choosing this reality, how noble you are. Over the long term, what this did to me was just deeply entrench to me that at worst, I was not worthy of success, and at best I did not want success, but my spirit did. Problem was the ill-disciplined thoughts were winning that battle hands down, and so my spirit became quiet, and I engaged in mundanity, all the while wondering what this existence was all about.

All this changed when I discovered and finally grasped the concept of awareness. Firstly though, it's worth remembering that I am not writing this journey from the vantage point of a teacher, just a guy discovering what I have. So there may be a much deeper definition of awareness out there, but to me, the simplicity of my perspective of it was mind-altering, especially since it had taken me this long to discover. Awareness is you in control, looking at your thoughts with curiosity instead of blind faith, cherry-picking the good ones from the bad ones, discarding them, laughing at them, honoring them, but most importantly, being in charge of them. Awareness is like a divine catalyst that leads you down the journey of questioning and creating instead of reacting and believing everything that your thoughts throw at you.

The initial liberation of this was groundbreaking for me and indeed was the spark of healing because I could now look at these disturbing thoughts that had put me here from afar. I could analyze then from a safe space of control, rather than the terror of them being remotely valid. This distance between my thoughts and I changed everything. This was my eye-of-the-tiger moment. While this new-found awareness needed developing, it was like divine dust moving through my consciousness, allowing me to begin to consider changing my story and engaging in spirit again. My new self was conceived. My job now was to nurture it to my redemption. This began with sitting down with my thoughts, a long-awaited board meeting, a hostile takeover where all the players would be named and responsibilities assigned.

Chapter 18

Boris

Now that I had grasped the concept that I had a built-in thought filter, my healing momentum gathered speed. The realization that the divine deemed it necessary to have this filter meant that clearly, my thoughts were suspect and needed parenting. This started to release the stomach ball of disgust that I had been living with because now for the first time, I was able to look at those thoughts with an air of curiosity and with increasing doubt.

The skill of awareness needed to be developed and became like a sort of mind gym. I would find myself giving my internal voice a talking-to after screaming at the person cutting in front of me in traffic. There were now two inner voices, which initially were overwhelming and loud, but this was a budding relationship and as such, we would need to cultivate our dynamic. The old self voice was not going to take the appointment of a new CEO lightly and initially became even more insistent, but at the same time, its utterances became even more ridiculous and quite frankly, bizarre. I came to see my thoughts as—if you pardon the expression—batshit crazy. I mean imagine the extreme change and turmoil going on when you are ceasing to trust yourself any longer. Even more sobering, the length of time you had trusted this internal Mad Hatter. This was so profound that I came to name my thoughts as *Boris*. Not sure why this choice

58

just seemed appropriate at the time. I still address my thoughts in that manner today.

Awareness, my new inner leader, would put Boris in his place when needed and oftentimes laugh outright at his suggestions. Boris came back fighting and tried to use every legacy tactic he had for the last fifty years. He would thrust the very thoughts that had put me in this place front and center, but this time, I would just observe and gently remind him that this was not me. I honored his pretensions, but politely and firmly dismissed them. Awareness was my new divine soldier and incredibly formidable. I was now in charge and could choose my thoughts, which in turn would temper my emotions. This new inner narrative relationship began flattening the hairs on my neck, which had been pretty much at attention this entire time. My throat began to unclog, and slowly, I began to feel my esteem begin to fight back. But even though I felt that I had begun to turn a corner, my newfound search for answers meant that I wanted to understand what had happened to me.

This is what I came up with. Again, forgive any simplicity, but the position that I was in meant that I needed to grasp concepts simply and take baby steps to becoming. With the stark realization that I had essentially backed myself into survival mode for my entire adult life, the fact that I had basically lauded scarcity meant that I had been bathing my insides with stress hormones for decades. This cannot be a healthy cocktail, and science has proven links to these hormones as major contributors to debilitating illnesses, both physical and mental in nature. The picture that I decided on was that my mind had just simply short-circuited, like a motherboard dropped in water, the synapses sparking and hissing, throwing out all sorts of jumbled code, spewing out madness. I had taken my brain through a stress hormone car wash one too many times, and on that day, it just said no more.

All of this intimacy of my chemicals meant that I was now steered into a new direction of inquiry. I needed a new shower, and I somewhat innately knew that my prescription was not enough. It felt more like me sticking my finger in a leak, a short-term solution. I began reading everything from Buddhists concepts to Dr. Joe

Dispenza telling me that I could become supernatural. These ideas were really out there for someone as pragmatic and as adamant as me, but they were littered with mind-boggling ideas. My developing awareness was asking me to be more open to ideas that normally I would have dismissed, and so began the next phase of my healing.

But first, I would have to get Boris under control again because he sensed that this doubt was indeed a chink in my armor. But the paradigm shift that was slowly moving away from life happening to me, toward me happening to life meant that Boris had his work cut out for him. I was beginning to take charge of my life and thoughts to actively navigate in a calm, considered way, moving away from the victim mentality into abundance and choice. I was now the rider of my chariot, steering Boris and asking him to change and come with me.

Awareness was like this door to a completely new way of thinking with all the prospects of being a divine reinvention. But I did still have my misgivings. My granite-like logic was not quite ready to bend yet, so while I had opened the door slightly, I would need to get out of my own way in order to fully walk through it.

Chapter 19

Skeptic

I mean, let's be real: the generation that I was born into had a very restricted point of view when it came to what is now amusingly called woo-woo. I was no different in this regard. My world and my existence were really black and white. You live, you die, and if you did okay, you went to heaven. I have always self-prescribed as spiritual, but what that really meant to me was that I did not identify with a specific religion, but rather the idea of living a good life and hopefully that would cement my place in the afterlife. This distinction was largely philosophical and was my easy throwaway when anyone asked about my religious convictions, but I did not engage in all of the potentials of being spiritual. My society had not ever really even offered any info other than be good, do good, and then pray.

So when Pamela started leaving books by Gabby Bernstein on my pillow, I was deeply skeptical. This for me was deep into the woo-woo realm. I pushed these books to the back of the queue and looked for books that were more pragmatic in their advice, books that I could relate to for the most part. Each night as I turned my bedside light off, there was Gabby screaming at me, "Yo, the universe has got your back." I would smirk and sleep. But here is the pesky thing about awareness: it operates your intuition, this language of the soul, steering you toward change, nudging you in directions that, given your own devices, you would never go near. This nagging little whisper that I should be open and just give it a go. The other curious thing that I began to notice was that the books that I began reading and that had been so responsible for my transformation all had their pom-poms out and were chanting the truth of the esoteric.

Reluctantly one evening, I picked up Gabby and began to read. Six hours later, I closed the cover; that book was simply devoured. I grabbed another. I began to follow Gabby on Instagram, which in itself was remarkable. All of this felt somehow like there was another internal pilot driving this adventure. The rational me was screaming that this stuff was just a little "out there" for me to embrace, but my spirit was listening. Gabby spoke of universal signs speaking to her, moments of real-time guidance she received from the universe at big and small junctures of her life. Like the time she wanted to buy a new house and had asked the universe to give her a sign that it was the right thing to do. The miracle of how that sign appeared to her and gave her the affirmation that she needed, even when she had all but decided that she was not going to receive that sign. She spoke of the concept of having access to some kind of divine tour guide to your life. This light-filled resource available and on tap to all of us who were open to developing the relationship.

To a disillusioned little Catholic boy, this was all so far out, but I had this odd mixture of trepidation and excitement growing in me. This was a tussle between my tried and tested and failed brand of rationality and the promise of new horizons was confusingly beautiful. I would sit for hours in traffic contemplating this. It was so far away from my construct that the skeptic in me was just not prepared to blindly accept it all. I needed irrefutable proof, a mathematical formula that would leave me in no doubt of the power of this new world. Thing is that things of this divine nature require a leap. They require faith, which in many ways has no logic which, to a fairly narrow-minded human, can be hard to grasp. I believed in God and had faith in that, but the thought that I could engage in reciprocated conversations with the divine on a daily basis was a monster paradigm.

There was only one thing really left for me to do. I needed to try out some of these concepts for myself and see if they had any credibility. I figured I would go straight for the jugular, so I started right at the place of the most resistance for me, so I started asking for...

Chapter 20

Signs

I started dipping my toe in the concept of a miracle morning; it meant starting my day with a small meditation and some writing of intention for the day ahead. The grand idea behind this was to begin really connecting with the divine, growing a real relationship with spirit. This was far more invested than the odd prayer I would mutter from time to time before wading off to dreamland, but it was also the small beginnings of taking control of my life, imprinting my thoughts with daily intention. I needed to be consistent and committed to this practice. Gabby had assured me that my investment would bring life-altering change. Having been at the bottom of the barrel, I was up for anything, even though the early stages of this shift were still with that niggling skeptic's heart.

I persevered and started seeing the benefits very soon; even if these early changes were more of a mechanical nature, they were still positive moves. I say mechanical because what began was that my early intentions would stay with me throughout the day, so I began acting in a way that would give those intentions the best chance of being. Since no one would create negative intentions, my disciplined approach had me acting in light, wanting my prescription to come true. I suppose the best way to sum it up is that I had begun to approach life differently, which could only have different results. This feeling of now having my hands on the steering wheel of my life was where the liberation began. I started creating my own personal mantras that would reverberate through me all day and replace the unhealthy irrational cruel ruminations with healthy ones. Things like *joy*, *love*, and *excellence* became my new soundtrack, and I danced to this new tune, changing the landscape of my life.

But through all of this, I was still able to explain these changes away as on more of a practical level. I was the change; there was nothing woo-woo about this. I made myself the champion, pretty typical really, and part of the past residue of my makeup. However, the internal dialogue had begun: my intuition was leading me toward a new insight, I was moving toward becoming a divine adopter, my skeptical shackles were falling away from inside, and my dormant spirit was rising. But I did still need something that would shake me to my core. I was yearning for the unexplainable. I needed a sign, just like the ones Gabby had spoken of as a regular companion to her life choices. I guess the only way to get this was to put it to the test. I followed the plan that I had read about. I meditated and asked the universe to reveal to me an animal, one that could be my sign indicator. I was given or decided—I was not sure of which at the time—birds of prey; eagles and hawks were my sign animal.

I began to actively engage in conversations with the universe. I would get totally specific. Like when I was driving to an interview to get some consulting work, I asked the universe to give me a sign that it was the right thing to do. I pictured seeing an eagle on a vehicle of sorts. My drive was about two hours, and I was looking at every passing vehicle to see any reference to an eagle. I saw nothing for the entirety of the trip. So much so that my mind wandered and I had all but forgotten about this by the time of my arrival. I decided to phone Pamela to let her know that I had arrived safely. I was totally preoccupied with this conversation, walking up and down the sidewalk chatting away, killing time because as usual, I had arrived beyond early. I walked past a motorbike numerous times without taking notice, until I did, and there on the gas tank was a beautiful picture of an eagle, parked right outside the building I had to walk into. I got the job and began believing in signs, right there.

Now I know the skeptics would say, if you think of a red car, you suddenly see red cars everywhere, and having been a staunch skeptic, I can see the argument. But here is the thing: I believe in God and have done for my entire life. I was never the most devout of people, but I believed. This in itself required a leap of faith; it required believing in the omnipresent, something bigger than us, something magical and all powerful. So it is not the biggest leap in the world to go to there being some divine intervention possible in our lives. I have never bought into the arrogance of man, that we are the highest order in this infinite universe. I believe in the spirit; I am spiritual as opposed to religious, but I believe. The thing is, I had never really engaged in a meaningful relationship with the spirit. I was too busy wrapped up in my own arrogance and story. My life had been so outward, caring so much about what the outside world's perception of me was. These are largely interruptive pursuits and really take you further away from the spirit. All of this turmoil had really made me look at my priorities and go on this journey of seeking, which was more and more inward as each day passed. This ultimately led me to begin a daily habit that has not only changed my life, but it was a hurdle that I was the most skeptical about and had ridiculed for years.

Chapter 21

Meditation

This one is the true magic of my recovery; it's like soul water. I only wish that I had not been so dogmatic in denying it for so long. My old self bathed in arrogance saw this as the exclusive practice of bead-wearing, flowing cotton shirt hippie types. I chose not to relate until people I could relate to were singing of its life changing powers. The desperation of my situation had taken me to a place of being willing to try anything. This, I now know, was the intention of the divine. It also has to be said that the world we live in today makes dipping your toe into meditation much easier than before. There are countless apps out there that offer guided meditations from any starting point. So this is where I began my journey, not really expecting much, but feeling good about acting.

While I was in the middle of profound discovery at this time and there had been some truly amazing concepts in that seeking, I was still stuck. My insides were clogged, had no movement, and stiff with the mindless repetition of the hamster wheel. My life process was full, spaceless. I was constantly living in either the past or the future. My nights would be plagued with regrets or some upcoming event to fix or solve. I had made the decision that getting up every day, and grinding against the wall of destiny would eventually, by sheer grit, bring me to my true purpose. I had put all my cards in on work ethic and relentless daily do-overs. Groundhog day at its finest—just waiting for the day when all of this drudgery would somehow miraculously change, and I would stand before my truth. But my truth was all of this constant mental unrest was just taking me further away from myself and dulling my resolve and bathing me in disappointment of never arriving. So now when I needed answers the most, I had none, but even worse, I was beginning to shatter my nobility, which was what had served as the glue to my mentality for this entire time.

So as I turned on the soothing tones of my beginner meditation instructor, I was throwing my Hail Mary. I was moving into a new realm out of my headspace into my heart space. My old self still stirs at me writing that—so foreign I was to emotion. Put simply, in order for me to get change, I would have to change, and this step inward was the first step. There was no major earth-shattering moment of realization these first times, but my budding intuition made me feel like this was a worthy adventure. I knew somehow instinctively that consistency would be the key to a new horizon. So I set myself a target of doing thirty uninterrupted days, made a little easier by the fact that these digital platforms give you courses to complete. I had, by this time, discovered commitment: ways past my normal procrastination which was the magic sauce in acting.

I whizzed through the thirty days, having the most profound sessions mixed with the mundane. But I looked forward to my sessions. This was the epitome of *me* time. I had discovered mindful quiet, blissful silence, space away from the demands of the life I had created. This glorious time to examine and engage in the unknown—and more importantly embrace my infinity—began to reveal to me new ways, new ideas. I was putting a deadbolt on the mindless repetition each day and inviting in the swirling colors of infinite possibility. Each day I would bask in my own spinning VR system, pouring color into me, around me. This energetic galaxy replaced the dread ball in my stomach with hope, big-picture hope…purpose.

My life could be so much bigger than these societal pursuits, the endless humdrum of trying to find my true life purpose. I started to create the foundations of a life beyond my dreams, indeed beyond my consciousness because here among the colors, there was freedom, no judgment. Here in my daily habit I could become anything. I was both limitless and insignificant. I started to feel a divine unclogging a beautiful release of my dread. I was now relating each day to my spirit, creating a new landscape with my eloquent mantras, and then on other days just sitting in the quiet, breathing, creating, and the biggest of all, discovering my worthiness. This new inner voice creating a narrative of belief and betterment left me feeling invigorated as opposed to exhausted. This divine imprinting of my conscious and subconscious mind began showing up in my daily actions. I was becoming, shedding my old self, and flourishing into the unknown. I trusted outcomes rather than trying to outsmart life; the universe has got it. Now not only was the energetic divine power revealed to me, but I had a hotline to its joy each day. I was the universe.

I began slowing down, looking at things from the view of my energetic fingerprint. What energy was I putting into the beauty and purity of that universe? Crazy thought. I even started listening more than talking. Those who know me may find that as hard to believe. But everything became about my impact in the stars and what my stardust was bringing to this parallel. I was letting go of things in a blink because I now knew how short this journey is. My perspective was changing. It was as if meditation had cleaned the window to reveal a paradise of limitless possibility. Once this image was seen, I could never go back. I was transformed, recreated, intentional, and ultimately, in charge of my choices in each moment. I pulled myself out of the past. I chose not to worry about the future and just live and be present in each moment. The ultimate irony: being that in the midst of my breakdown I had reduced my life to moments to survive, now here I was, living in those same moments in order to thrive. It was just a question of mindset. Full circle indeed.

Each time I found myself drifting into tomorrow and its problems, I began just telling my thoughts, *Those are for another moment*, which would bring me into the now. Being so present just meant that all I needed to do was choose how to use or be in that moment. It became startlingly logical: if I could sprinkle these moments with goodness with happiness with the positive, then I could, just by glorious presence, change my entire paradigm to be naturally positive.

This laser attention to the now brought life into small purposeful steps. No big-picture worries, no five-year plans, just the now. What is my choice now? This began to truly create change in my life. My only regret is having found the gift of meditation so late.

What this practice has made me is a seeker and a creator. I had a daily safe place in the stillness, where I could explore my mistakes, my desires, and most importantly, my actions. In order to change my life, I would have to change. This, by default, meant that I would need to embrace the new, the unknown, be excited, and trusting of things I knew nothing about. Once again leaps of faith were required. Meditation gave me the foundation of a deep knowing that the universe did indeed have my back. After all, we connected every day. This daily life change gave me another ingredient that I had left behind in my commitment to drudgery and repetition. It turns out that this part of the recipe is the spark that lights the gas of change and is my daily companion, my filter.

Chapter 22

Curiosity

Facades are false. We all have them to one degree or another from trying to fit in, in the playground to the perils of high school all the way to our ultimate public faces we show to the world. The pressure of society and wanting to be seen as successful led me down a road of highly evolved mask-wearing. When I was at the height of my professional masquerading, I was living in the city of Cape Town. This city is the jewel of South Africa, splendid in its white beaches, mansion-draped coastline, and the endless supply of fast cars and beautiful bodies. It is a place where outward status symbols are the most prized currency, a place where people drive convertibles and Range Rovers and never invite you back to their studio apartments. Everything is appearance. Toned physiques and model looks are a dime a dozen. Being on the VIP list at the latest flash in the pan club will give you a throng of friends, looking for the access.

I started a business in this place, my first foray into the business world. I had a celebrity clientele, and most of the IT crowd frequented my store. Anyone on the outside looking in would say I was brilliantly successful, except I wasn't. I lived in the terrifying grip of cash flow, or the lack thereof every single month. By the standards of the starkness of a balance sheet, I was insolvent, but sadly, there was no way at the time that I was ready to admit that to myself, and certainly not to the greater shiny community. So I masked myself and my business in a gold tinted facade. I drank at VIP tables, all the while giving away my product at a sickeningly reduced price to get the right people sitting in the front window of my store. I lived in fakery every day, so much so that I had myself believing my own hype.

Reality and story co-mingled until I did not know or did not want to know what was actually real. I superglued my insides and dove into the narrative of that's my story and I am sticking to it. I waded into the quicksand of keeping up with the Joneses and soon found myself stuck. This inertia of four steps forward and then four steps back glued me to no progress. The hamster wheel of repetition gripped me with a smirk of monotony, but real success—living a truthful abundant life—always eluded me. I explained it away as just not being my time, all the while living and probably believing the lie and putting on my public face day after day.

The casualty of this was curiosity. Being stuck in the routine of a facade meant that I questioned nothing. I had no bandwidth to really ask the big questions. I committed completely to painting a picture for the world. It meant I bought cars I could not afford. I cultivated healthy lumps of credit card debt all because I wanted the world to see me in a fabricated light. I had no courage to present myself, warts and all, to society. I wanted to be a jock. I wanted my name to be whispered with reverence in the bleachers. I wanted to be popular at any price. I created my story and I rode it hard. I defined myself by it, all the while sending my spirit, my silver thread to true purpose deep into that chest that I locked away. That wonderful trick of my brand of masculinity used with the expertise of a quarterback: avoid, lock away, and forget—easy.

But here is the thing: our spirit—I believe anyway—is the divine spirit within us. We are eternal and are sent through a journey of discovery in order to graduate into our places in eternity. This spirit is our North star, our intuition, a lighthouse in the storms of the human experience. It is bathed in free will and does not seek to decide our navigation, but rather let us progress along the spiritual plain or come back until we do. Our actions either take us closer to spirit, or further away from it. It ultimately becomes our choice.

This human construct and all its contrivances are really just one huge self-improvement course. Our grade at the end will be how justly and honestly we lived it. Our worldly legacy at the end will just simply be what kind of human you were. The Rolls-Royce will mean nothing but an item on your will to be fought over.

So if meditation provided me a safe place where I could go inward and really look at my story, my masks, and the state of my spiritual legacy, curiosity was the gasoline for me to change. This naked elixir was the tonic to get me unstuck, the strength to recraft my story. This time, to build my frequency on truth and to ask the right questions, no matter how hard the answers. Meditation and curiosity were the salt and pepper of my new relationship with spirit, the first steps in creating a recipe of abundance. My plate was over-flowing with potential, satiating my appetite for a graduation legacy! It was here in this soup of nude honesty and awakening that I discovered the first and most critical pillar of abundance.

Chapter 23

Purpose

Growing up as a kid, I played in countless Wimbledon finals, world cups where I routinely scored hat tricks which included the winning goal. I even knocked Sugar Ray Leonard out to get the championship belt. I did all of this in the comfort of my backyard because as we all know, kids dream, and they do it freely without constraint. There is no complication or self-developed restraint that reigns in those dreams. They are vibrant and lucid, the innocence of childhood. I suppose I could say that one of the great tragedies of the social system we have created is simply that it kills this dream freedom. As we get more and more indoctrinated with duty and responsibility, whether we like it or not, our dreams fade into necessity. Reality is the great yoke of our life process.

For me, all of those dreams were about impact and being some-one. Sure, they were somewhat naive considering my level of sporting prowess. But somewhere deep inside even at that age, I understood the concept of purpose. I gravitated to dreaming of the extraordinary. I practiced my interviews over and over in my head. In that shiny world of dreams, I was polished, revered, and most of all, there was a purpose and an imprint that I had on this world. All so far away from the mundanity and monotony of livelihood and providing. These dreams were electric, pulsating with reason: the joy of a life filled with purpose and impact, even though it only existed in my head.

Then as I grew, so, too, did the expectations from all sides: the dread of report cards, the lesson of chores. Life became filled with measurement and future pressure. By default, as this took hold, my dreams became tamed and more tempered. They were now painted with practicality and reality, and so by comparison, they dulled until they were forgotten. As with anything not practiced, I actually think I completely lost the skill of dreaming as adulthood, and self-realization kicked in. I willingly jumped on the hamster wheel and did what we are supposed to do: engage in society in an upstanding way and fulfill your duties to society. My only purpose really was kind of like an empty survival: pay the rent, pay the staff, rob Peter to pay Paul, all the while trying to present the image of togetherness to the world. I had a practiced smile, a well-trained demeanor. For most observers, I was doing good.

Sure, at times along this journey, I would snatch at purpose and mentor someone to help them down their career path. I would quietly congratulate myself and convince myself that this was my reason, my life purpose. But for a kid with such grandiose dreams, this seemed a little underwhelming. This is the insidious byproduct of being fully entrenched in survival mode. It makes you lower your gaze, put the blinkers on, and really sacrifice your dreams. You watch as a member in the stands as people live their best lives and explain it away as some kind of universal luck, and since you have never won anything in your life, you just accept your lot and grind on. Never once during all of this did I ever once consider that I could make a shift and manufacture my best life, so I waited and waited for that break. Look, universe, I have done everything right. My parking tickets are paid; I am law-abiding—pick me. Let me ride along my dreamscape. Oh, how I waited.

Only by going on this journey did I truly discover that dreaming is critical and should always be encouraged all the way into old-hood. Dreaming is abundant thinking. It should be huge. Dream the biggest things, pepper your subconscious with all the wonderment it can handle, and let life and all its wonderful possibilities pulsate through your being. Thrown into all of this cosmic dancing, I think all of us want to matter. We want to leave a spiritual legacy behind, a memory of who we were. This for me has truly begun to take root in the deep internal investigation of purpose. By finding my true purpose and driving toward it, I am infusing my life with an intoxicating cocktail that jumps off the humdrum wheel and dives into the sea of meaning.

Purpose is the first pillar—for me anyway—of building a solid foundation to an abundant life. I mean if I can get up every day and engage in my purpose, my reason for being, then surely my life becomes more blessed, more worthy, and here I feel the sweet tendrils of abundance creep into my life process. This is not wrapped around the material trappings, but more of why am I here and am I fulfilling my purpose? So for me, I had to take a step toward purpose. I mean, this book is all about taking action toward purpose. If my journey helps someone out there enduring the cold lonely nights of mental health, that right there is the Rolls-Royce of purpose.

It's that drive toward abundance that has me sitting here at 3:00 a.m. writing because it's in action that my purpose begins to live. It's here while everyone sleeps that I sign the contract of dreaming again, that I switch from existing to living. It's here that I see the speck of abundance on the horizon, my new beacon of trust and action. One step at a time. Take hold of my purpose. Keep building those pillars one day at a time. Make abundance a choice, not a lottery ticket. Build your first pillar of purpose because the second one, I hope, is where the real magic happens.

Chapter 24

Service

I think that once you have been to the depths of despair that a mental health crisis takes you to, the natural response is service. The healing that it offers is the opportunity of rebirth. It makes your suffering worth it. For me hand in hand with purpose, service offered me something beyond the man-made obstacle course and deeper into eternal. This grand perspective of why we are truly here and the human construct is really just our spiritual examination. Our place in the stardust of eternity is determined by how we navigate this dimension. This is the truth of legacy, a deep and meaningful imprint that at its core has the service of others as its beacon. It's in this survival that spirit dances in glee, and this celebration brings great winds of healing into the soul. In some way, I felt I needed to suffer in order to change my focus from the worldly to the eternal.

The mutterings of service started in me in a very lofty way. My images were of me standing on stages telling my story. Resonating with my audience and shooting out the elixir of hope, serving all: there is a way, you are not alone, go deep inward, learn how to feel again, and open those locked chests that you put away. Look at your life and take control of your story and blaze a new course, one of your own making, cherry-picking all of the good parts of your imprints and discarding the bad ones. Build who you want to be instead of just merely accepting who you were made. I would muse about my service being a worldly impact. I would sit with Gabby on her podcast, reaching thousands of ears, allowing men to realize how much of a strength vulnerability is. I wrote this book as a means of service, not from the point of view of a self-help guru, but really a real struggle and how I survived it and then turned it into thriving.

But after all of this daydreaming, I realized something that has created a concrete more critical change in my life. Start the steps of service, take action, and start serving at home or at work. Serve deep in the arms of obscurity, serve my son by being a more present dad, serve my wife by being all that I can be for her, and the list goes on and on. Opportunities to serve surround us. As I started to identify those daily opportunities and then acted on them in a completely selfless way, I started to repair. My light began to shine. My insides were smiling while my veins pulsated with purpose. Such a simply noble pursuit. Do for others, smile at strangers, lend a listening ear, and be free with hugs! Whatever it is, our spirit flourishes when we do good. It makes us feel good. We help humanity. There can be no bigger service than this. The things we do in the unseen: no celebrations, no book launches, no podcasts—just pure day-to-day service. This is true healing!

Discovering or re-remembering service has changed me. I have grown in a friendship with myself. I have felt the tight grip of self-loathing loosen, my self-esteem fighting back, each punch of humility in service giving me a shot of light legacy. Now through surrender and courage I have access to all I need for me to change the self-destruction construct and drink the tonic of growth and change. It was here in the intentional daily navigation that I discovered the third pillar in this divine trifecta, the grease that ignites purpose and service, something so gloriously simple in its application, but so profound in its result...

Chapter 25

Gratitude

One of the truly transformative ideas that I found in all of the books I read came in the form of the power of now. Simply put, the idea is simply that the past is gone. The future does not exist, so all we have is this moment, and if we bring our lives into just focusing on this present moment and choosing how you spend it, this is the eye of true self power. Sometimes, to me anyway, the way the world and all its gurus have sold all of the trappings that come with getting closer to spirit have at times been overladen with drippings of the esoteric. While I am a true believer and such esoteric, woo-woo does not scare me. I think it can render the message and its benefits more niche than mass market.

If I look at my path and my intentional avoidance of these things, I explained it all away as the domain of the hippies and did not subscribe to that niche. Now sure, this assessment was laced in judgment and hugely to my detriment. I believe if the idea was put in a more layperson format, I would have gravitated much sooner. Simply, my logic needs to be engaged. Let me outline a logical concept that struck me once I began practicing gratitude daily which brought me into the moment. What does this moment mean to me right now? Being so in tune with the moment made me realize the beautiful simplicity of mastering our own lives.

So take the idea of abundance, which more often than not is wrapped up in the grand idea of manifestation. See it, believe it, and it will come to pass. I agree this is an overly simplistic description of manifesting, but it was kind of the sales pitch that I had seen. I scoffed at this idea because I felt like it did not ever take into account the random unfairness of life, which was made even more laughable because this message was normally being peddled by someone with a far grander life than mine. I was stuck on the treadmill of obscurity, visualizing things to death, and my groundhog existence did not ever change dramatically. Full admittance: I was deeply cynical and had, in some sense, surrendered to my lot in life. Then as this journal of healing outlines, the universe decided to take me inward and cultivate the courage to question all things, but most importantly, from the vantage point that my views and philosophies were probably wrong. Allowing my ego to be snubbed and overrun by humility opened myself to reexamination.

This opening of my insides led me to staying in the moment, making a concerted effort to be in the here and now. Before all of this, my life had been spent lamenting the past and trying to control the future. I was living my life in a permanent state of rewind and fast forward, and my emotional state reflected that blur. I was oscillating between *woe is me* and *when will my lucky break roll in?* Days turned into months into years into decades. These two forces were in control, the puppet masters of the ordinary. But here is the logic of living in the moment and the practice of gratitude, and in keeping with form and trying to make this digestible and even better approachable, I will keep it obscenely simple. If you take control of the present moment and you actively and intentionally charge that moment with positivity for the most part, then by simple mathematics, your life-spent ratios become more positive than negative and or indifferent. So if you are able to have a ratio like 70 percent positive moments to 30 percent negative moments, this by default would equal a life of abundance in its purest form.

The simple step into this blissful logic is to control what you can in each moment. Live today to your fullest, roll with the unknown and break life down to now, and take charge of your present response. Then no matter what your social standing or aspirations, you can pepper your life with contentment and happiness and come to realize the simple little momentary things are the true measurement of success, a success that has more to do with your standing in the eternal than it does in that fading new car smell. A smile, a hug, a warm meal, family, digging your toes into wet beach sand—these things have way more value than that promotion or wristwatch. To live your life in the presence of joy is the truth of a life of abundance, and the guest list is just simply looking for the good and being grateful for the daily opportunities we all have to connect to meaning.

Once I had grasped this idea and slowly built up the muscle memory of it becoming a habit, I felt that dread ball in my stomach release its grip. This to me was the step into embracing the unknown and taking charge of my responses, making them considered, more evolved. Change started happening. I gave my son more hugs. I reacted way more calmly to adversity. I became more of an attractive light than a dark cloud, and it is here that the path is paved for miracles to happen, like the winds of life change bringing with them peace and growth. All of this by the simple intentional act of gratitude, being thankful— remarkably concise! The problem is, however, that we live in a social system that breeds wanting. We are reared in comparison and bombarded by messages of things we want but don't have. A subject for another book, but social media has become a digital virus, comparison fodder on instant demand at our fingertips all hours of the day. These carefully curated illusions only succeed in making us feel our lives are so inadequate. After all, as we scroll, we see people living their ultimate lives, while we slog through the mundane demands of life.

This constant comparison does not lead to gratitude. In fact, quite the opposite. We spend our lives hankering, always looking for it to be better, to be different than the one we actually have. I bought into this hook, line, and sinker. It led me to workaholism, drinking the Kool-Aid, wishing myself to a new life, a life like that person I just saw on the gram. But once I had truly committed to being present in the moment—first as a means of survival, and then as a method of thrival—I began to see blessings. I realized just how lucky I am to be living my life. This is true healing, and I am grateful for gratitude every day.

Chapter 26

Now

Today, now I am different. I am changed. Let's say more educated. My crisis sent me to a school of sorts, and desperation is a wonderful motivator. Best I can simplify: what I have come to adopt as a new mindset through all of the wonderful teachers out there producing works about subjects that were in some way taboo for my generation and gender. Our minds are on a default setting of survival: legacy of the chance of a wooly mammoth stampede, as we have evolved the brains basic idea of safety has not, but we have evolved into something totally foreign to that loincloth-wearing cave man of our ancestors. So the modern-day brain is wired to consider everything through a filter of caution, which in my mind manifests for us into habits that play to that caution. When we look at everything through the lens of skepticism, our overall mindset is, at best, comfortable with scarcity and, at worst, completely negatively wired. Our basic instinct is to be risk averse. We seek out habits and lifestyles that are safe. We choose not to be stretched in our thinking. This to me is how the greater society lives. We photocopy each other's life processes because monotony and repetition are safe. This allows our overly anxious mindsets to create some comfort for us, and we slide into these comfort zones, often and certainly in my case wondering, *Is this it? Is this life?*

We watch as eager spectators as we see others create a life that surpasses our own. Social media bombards us with others living their best lives, or at least appearing so. This constant diet of the different levels of life available to us being so much more than ours can create havoc in our own self-analysis. But as I chose to look deeper into my life and to analyze why I thought the way I did, I came to one very stark realization. The vast majority of us are living in our default mode of survival and have not yet discovered the idea of abundance simply because this journey requires us to step out of our deeply entrenched comfort zones.

To flick the switch of our minds that are so stubborn in their instincts, from scarcity to abundance, requires nothing more than evolving. We quite simply have to change the way our minds think. We have to obliterate the mold of history and imprint. We have to become not only comfortable with risk and the unknown, we have to love and embrace and dare to be all that we can be! This is by no means an easy thing to do. Breaking any cycle will always have a byproduct of challenge and sobering discovery, but the prize is true self-contentment and even more powerful self-trust. These are the antidote to anxiety and depression because they wrap you in the warmth of self-worth. They furnish you with the point of view of liking what you see in the mirror. This to me is the essence of fulfillment. I have learned to honor feelings of self-loathing and look at them objectively, but once I have looked them dead in the eye, I have foresight and courage to pay them no heed.

Look, I am not trying to paint a picture here of rainbow and roses all the time, but what I am trying to say is that self-discovery and an on-tap relationship with divine means the bad days are handled and accepted, and there are many more days of rainbows simply because you have created a new default: rose-tinted lenses that see this world as a wonderful playground of discovery. Your strength is deep within you. The universe, God lives deep in you, and if you create the habit of connecting daily with this source, this relationship flourishes and becomes your safe shore—your place of excitement, your realization that this life is just a distraction, a test of what you place value you in.

This crazy world we live in never ceases. Emails come at all times of the day. The constant pinging of demanding digital platforms really just bombard our psyche. It's no wonder mental unhealth is as prevalent as it is. I have found that the most valuable tool I have is to stop and breathe, sit still in quiet, and sit at the feet of the divine source and bathe in the swirling light of love and healing. These little divine breaths I take each day wash my mentality with safety and love, allowing me to puff out my chest and take this world and push toward optimization and be the best me I can be.

I am different today because I changed my mind. I put the work in every day and can look back at the shocking divine intervention that had me questioning living. And today I look at it as a blessing because without it, I would not have the universe as my suit of armor, and I would be engaged in a life of process living for the weekends, surviving and not thriving. It is hard and the habits of comfort are a worthy foe, but I have to understand the stakes. What am I going to pass on? What are going to be the consequences of my imprint? What is my legacy?

These are the things of an abundant mind I work every day to evolve. This journey started with me thinking somewhere that I was not a good enough man, husband, father. A terrifying concept, a tainted legacy that subconsciously I did not want life with. Mr. Divine stopped me in my tracks, with the simple message of go inward, fight, and surrender. Do whatever it takes to change course, find truth, and then live it every day. Change your mind, seek happiness and not monotony, seek self-discovery and not couch potato ambivalence, live in the spirit and be a good man, knowing that once you find the universal force, you simply cannot be stopped with the fuel of the divine, and it's right there inside all of us. We just need to take the time to nurture it.

Chapter 27

Tomorrow

So this is the dream, the reason why all of this happened. This complex divine intervention has to bring me to my reason, my purpose that will be my legacy in the light. In order for me to come full circle, I have to make it all count. I have to go from the depths of struggle to the glorious survival of meaning, so here in the last chapter, I am going to state my intention. All of my daily conversations with the universe, source, God—whatever you prefer to call this force that lives within us all—and once the relationship is truly cultivated, your real path and your galactic legacy is revealed, and all the angelic soldiers conspire to make it all a reality, carving your name into the tree of abundance and giving this life true, true meaning.

So for starters, I want to serve. My grand hope is that my journey can resonate and relate with anyone who may read it, that it may spur a new conversation around the brand of manhood that many of my generation and before carry. This rigid definition of strength and pushing things away deep and suffering in silence is the hardest of self-inflicted burdens to carry. I heard the other day of a crazy stat where a man dies by his own hand every minute in America. Ponder that for a second; something is wrong.

Now as I am in the middle of my own generation gap, trying to make sense of a world that my son is going to have to navigate, a world as foreign to me as the one my own parents had seen me have to navigate. The pressure for me to give him a tool set that will help him make his way in the world, a tool set so far removed from arithmetic and social studies. I want to give him a smorgasbord of skills for which to navigate things like anxiety, panic intolerance, and so many of the very prevalent issues of our time. The last thing I want to pass onto him is a brand of manhood that gives him nowhere to go but putting on a brave face and becoming so practiced in that skill that he builds a wall between him and himself.

How do I do this in a world where the very core of his self-esteem will be wrapped in likes and subscribers, a world where people feel free and so emboldened to say the most hideous things from behind an Instagram moniker? This digital landscape where he will have no choice but to live in the most cowardly and brutal of terrains. So far removed from the childhood that I lived. My frame of reference is so outdated with the world he lives in that if I just blindly pass on my imprint, he will start in the world as a relic and will just repeat the mistakes which I have made. I want to teach him that there is as much strength in surrender as there is in fight. I want to show him how vulnerability is probably the greatest strength of all. I want him to know how to ask for help and to give it as well as receive it. I want him to be able to cry without shame. I want him to have the courage to go inward and truly get to know himself. I want him to appreciate the moment and live in it because it is the only place of any real value. I want him to have less sleepless nights than me, tossing in the arms of insecurity and stress. I want him to have the freedom to live his life the way he sees fit, without the need to bask in the misguided nobility of being the only provider. In short, I want a different brand of man for him, the one that I have happened on halfway through my life, free from judgment and self-loathing, but rich with contentment and self-value. I want him to laugh more. I want him to love more. I want him to tolerate more. I want more for him and his generation.

But here is the real rub: the high-wire act of being a dad in these times, there has to be a mindful navigation through the old-school values and the new-school landscape. You see, I think we are losing some of the greatest attributes that were handed down from the generations before us. Things like integrity and respecting the ability to tolerate and accept differences. Society today is way too offended, and the digital world is uncontrolled and lacks a moral compass. It was only the other day that I saw a person online who self-described as a person of God, and then virtually in the same sentence expounded on the virtues and need for a *civil war* in America. I myself have been directly in the path of two such wars that no one ever won.

How have we gotten so off kilter? How have we gotten so far away from basic humanity. My belief is that we have created a life process that has moved us away from having a relationship with our maker. We feel we are free to sow seeds of hate into the light. This is not the world I want for my son, or anyone else for that matter. We need to cherry-pick from our past generations and bring back things like accountability, manners, real freedom, and most of all, tolerance. The simple goal is to just be good humans.

For me, the fact that I have created a life day-to-day, within which I commune with the universe every day, and not in a man-made confined or traditional way, but in a way where I am accepted just for me, warts and all. My God does not judge me, but rather gives me a place to go, a place of still and quiet where I can explore truth and legacy and where I am guided to who I want to be as a man. My meditations are like having a drink at the bar with a life-time friend, one who has seen all that I have or have not been, but loves me anyway, one who puts an arm around love no matter what, and then cajoles me to become.

So rounding this off, I am no scientist who can go into the vagaries of what happens to the brain when we choose to rewire it into a positive default. All I can do is be a witness to what I have been through and use it to help others. No matter how this comes, whether I have the privilege of speaking to a mass platform and being a soldier in arms, or if this testimony only touches one person, that will be a purpose found and a purpose lived. Even better that my son goes into the world happy in his own skin, drenched in self-trust and the ability to be strong in all the right ways, to honor and flush stress hormones from ravaging his insides and has a place just like mine to go to where he can freely explore his cause and purpose and be wrapped in the arms of the divine.

Thanks for reading.

About the Author

Nick is a husband and a father living in Temecula, California. He has lived and worked in three continents. Having been born in Africa, he came to the USA in search of the American dream.

For most of his life, he has had the goal of writing a book and having it published. Now in his early fifties, he found that book through a deep inward journey. He now wants to share it with the world in the hope that it will help to accelerate his ultimate goal, which is to live out his purpose of serving and hopefully helping others.

His journey into understanding the strength of being open and redefining the way he sees his own brand of manhood made it possible for him to release such a personal account to the world.

Printed in the USA
CPSIA information can be obtained
at www.ICGtesting.com
LVHW071324180923
758289LV00003B/468